Polly
A White German Shepherd Dog

Polly
A White German Shepherd Dog

D. Brian Plummer

PERRY
GREEN
PRESS

British Library Cataloguing-in-Publcation Data
A catalogue record for this book is available from
the British Library

ISBN 1 902481 04 6

Typeset by Adrian McLaughlin

Front cover image © Julie Hindle

Printed in Great Britain by Redwood Books, Trowbridge

Contents

Introduction

It would be ludicrous for me to claim to be an expert on the subject of the German Shepherd Dog. It would also be a false claim. I have never shown a dog of any breed in my life. Indeed I should feel vaguely embarrassed if asked to take a dog into the show ring in an attempt to tempt a judge into saying that my dog was more beautiful than the others. I know something, though not much, about the conformation the German Shepherd Dog standard suggests is ideal, although I am bewildered at the sight of people attempting to show this breed of dog. The sight of young men and women, and all professional German Shepherd Dog handlers seem to be quite young, being towed around a show ring by a wilful and powerful beast at speeds akin to those set up at the White City Greyhound Stadium, is faintly irritating. In fact, it is my belief that a dog subjected to this form of mental conditioning would be a devil incarnate to train to any level of obedience after its stint in the show ring. Yet the breed council is about to initiate working tests for these wild and beautiful show dogs so that they might be classed as dual purpose animals.

It is in fact amazing that the people who show German Shepherd Dogs are often totally inept at producing an animal that is obedient and well behaved out of the show ring, as the breed is the most biddable of animals, capable of performing the most exacting of tasks if properly trained – and the expression properly trained is one that must be considered carefully. Colonel Baldwin who was a great enthusiast of the German Shepherd Dog, or Alsatian as it was called at that time, once stated that the breed was either the best of dogs or the worst of dogs, depending on how it was trained, or more important still, who was training the animal.

In the right hands the beast becomes an excellent family dog, a fine protective police dog, a tracker dog with a nose rivalling that of the bloodhound, a drug detection dog, a guide dog for the blind, a listening dog for the deaf, a sniffer dog able to detect narcotics even thought they are sealed in plastic bags or explosives equally well concealed. The German Shepherd Dog is the most versatile of animals, able to detect the presence of corpses and injured people amidst bomb-damaged rubble, able to find travellers buried in snow drifts with an alacrity which puts the traditional St. Bernard to shame. Some German Shepherd Dogs will herd sheep and drive cattle although perhaps not as well as would a purpose bred Border collie which gathers up sheep with an almost surgical precision and with an unwholesome, excited expression on its wild-eyed black and white face. In fact, in the right hands the German Shepherd Dog is capable of learning any task. In the wrong hands – well, the German Shepherd Dog becomes an unwholesome nuisance, a stubborn disobedient brute and unmitigated pest or danger to all who encounter it.

Sadly my first experience with the German Shepherd Dog was with the latter kind. At the age of ten I obtained a part-time Saturday job working for a local grocer, for the use of child labour was common just after World War II. As a result of being a Johnny Come Lately, the last child to be employed, I was given the task of delivering goods to farms quite distant from the shop, farms so out of the way, so off the beaten track, that the owners of such premises had developed that almost terrifying quaintness, a mixture of the characters straight out of the works of George Elliot and H. E. Bates perhaps. One would insist that I unloaded each item from my grocery box, placing each tin, jar or package on the doorstep while he watched me through the letterbox uttering phrases such as, 'Didn't want that', 'That's no good', before passing the money to me through the same letterbox. I delivered to this farm for two years yet I never actually met the gentleman who placed the grocery orders. Once I watched from some distance away in an attempt to observe him gathering up the groceries, but shy as a bush baby, he refused to take the bait until he heard my heavy grocer's bike groan and clatter off down the lane. I'm rambling again, the prerogative of an ageing man, so I shall return to my tale.

During the two years I worked as a grocer's boy I learned much of canine behaviour. In fact I'm surprised retired postmen don't set themselves up as 'dog behaviour modification' experts (a somewhat grandiose title), for after twenty or so years of running canine gauntlets they must acquire a great knowledge of the behaviour of dogs in order to survive their rounds.

Prior to my spell on the grocery round my knowledge of dogs had been confined to my pet terriers and to the noble, sagacious dog found in literature, or seen on the screen at our local cinema. These fictional dogs were fabulous beasts, loyal to masters, capable of distinguishing legitimate visitors from those with evil intentions and acting accordingly. They were in fact a far cry, or star's flight, from the vicious beasts I sometimes met on my delivery round.

My Shaitan, my Nemesis, call him what you will, was a wall-eyed pale blue merle collie who stalked me as would a lion a gazelle, quivering with excitement as it did so, drooling slightly, an unwholesome look in its apparently blind wall eyes. Indeed it is a popular misconception that wall or white eyes are more defective than normal coloured eyes. It would wait until I opened the farm gate, secreting itself amongst the bales of straw, stealthily slithering towards me on its belly, making use of the rubbish and antique farm machinery which littered the yard to hide behind until I closed the gate and was unable to escape. The brute would then race forward and put in a half-hearted though bruising bite to my calves before knocking me flat and staring into my face with these apparently blind, yet all-seeing pale blue eyes. At first the brute terrified me – although I would have been more terrified still if I had realised the damage a bite from a demented collie could inflict, but long before my twelfth birthday, when an appendectomy caused me to lose my job, I had realised that the stalking, the feigned attack and the staring into the face of the downed victim was simply a ritual, a ritual as predictable as a Catholic Mass, the dog had chosen to evolve and, like most rituals, did not alter a great deal in the way both the dog and I were expected to perform. The beast continued to bite with the same half-hearted force, never breaking the skin, never biting my face once it downed me and after a while I entered into the spirit of the ritual, seeking out a soft spot on which to be felled and not moving a muscle until the dog decided it was time to allow me to rise. After acting out this game the beast would wag its tail and joyfully accompany me to the farmstead where I delivered the groceries. It would be a lie to say that I developed an affection for the brute or made a friend of the dog, but when an outbreak of hard pad – a form of distemper which caused the dog's pads to harden until the dog clatters like a Walt Disney horse – reduced the dog to a 'fitting' pathetic wreck, I felt some sadness at the demise of the beast. In fact my foe was to be replaced by a greater terror when the owner of the antique collie speculated some ten pounds and purchased a virtually fully grown German Shepherd Dog, or Alsatian as it was were referred to at that time, called Arno.

The War Time years, the food rationing and the meatless diet of those dogs, had meant that few large and exotic breeds were kept in the village. I can still remember my excitement when I spied a Chow Chow, recognisable only by dint of reference to Doggie Hubbard's 'Observer's Book Of Dogs', in the company of an off-white Samoyed at a dog show at our local Ambulance Hall. Hence with some excitement I visited Mr Webb's farmyard to see his most recent purchase – a fully-grown black and tan German Shepherd Dog.

***

I have always been reluctant to take on a second-hand dog, a dog which has experienced much of the formative period of its life in the company of another owner. Why the owner wishes to part with such a beast is also a little questionable, for few half-grown or sapling dogs are sold for anything like the cost of the purchase price and rearing a dog to such an age can be a very costly business. Sometimes saplings are sold simply because they have not grown into the aesthetically pleasing creatures exhibitors expected – and they are then passed on to other owners at less that the price it would cost to purchase an eight week old uninoculated whelp.

Other half-grown dogs change hands when the couple who have bought the puppy decide to separate, and it is not a little surprising how many dog owning couples decide to separate and divorce, and because neither now have a permanent home and are leading lives best described as being 'in a state of flux', decide to part with the whelp. Dogs that change hands after a marital upheaval are seldom good prospects I must add. The constant bickering and warring that usually precedes a marital break-up has an unsettling effect on any breed of dog and the young animal usually arrives at its new home in a somewhat confused state. Dogs are in fact the mirrors of what is going on in the household.

Yet there is usually a more sinister reason why half-grown dogs of any breed, particularly the larger, more powerful breeds, change hands. Perhaps the reader will now forgive a digression so early in the book – although I confess I must control the habit if I am to continue as a writer. A puppy enters into the human family or pack at the epsilon or bottom most level. In the canine pack an epsilon animal will accept the attentions, hostility and aggressive behaviour of the rest of the pack without retaliation and seemingly without complaint, for the average puppy willingly gives way to any dog which intimidates it. The puppy entering the human pack at the epsilon level must learn to accept its position and, more important still, never try to elevate itself in the social structure of the said family. It must tolerate without complaint the torment and love (and often the brutality) meted out by the smallest child – and children can often be very cruel to dogs – without retaliation. It should in fact be at home in its epsilon position and should be kept in that position by the entire family. I have little doubt that the man in the street knows precious little about canine behaviour and will certainly not notice the telltale signs that the dog is trying to elevate its position in the family's social hierarchy. The chances are that the head of the family, man or woman, will find the sight of a newly bought puppy jealously guarding its food dish, growling and snarling when it is approached, slightly amusing and will not try to correct this antisocial behaviour. Thus by the time the puppy begins to resent intrusion in its sleeping area or be a shade too protective about its favourite chair or rug, the dog has elevated itself out of the epsilon position in the family and is dangerously out of control. It is now only a matter of time before the now very disturbed and potentially dangerous animal snaps at one of the family. If the dog is very small – a toy breed for instance – the consequences of such behaviour are slight – although there is certainly worse to follow. If the dog is a large one, or of a breed specifically tailored to be a guard dog – a German Shepherd Dog, Dobermann or Rottweiler – the result of such an attack on a child can be horrendous.

Funnily enough the sort of person most likely to buy one of these large, powerful dogs with a tendency to elevate itself up the social scale at the expense of the rest of the family, is usually a rather weak, epsilon type man. Thus a marriage in Hell is made – the union of a large, powerful dog (few bitches are keen on attempting to move up the social hierarchy in a human family/pack) and a weak rather silly owner who has probably bought the animal to elevate his own position in the human tribe ('Gosh, look at that man with the huge dog.').

I believe that Webb, the farmer, acquired the dog Arno (all German Shepherd Dogs in South Wales at this time seemed to be called Arno after the success of Ch. Arno of Saba no doubt) simply because the dog's previous owner had lost control of the animal and the beast had started to dominate the family, perhaps savaging anyone who dared offend it. It was quite a large male and slightly nervous to boot, but it lost no time in establishing itself in its new home at the Alpha level and began to tyrannise Mr Webb, a retired school teacher who had opted out of teaching once he realised he had no ability to control a class of fairly placid valley children.

He certainly had no ability and possibly little inclination to control the large and powerful Arno. I made my delivery the day after Arno's arrival and confess I was utterly captivated by the dog's appearance. He was the first Alsatian I had seen in the flesh and had an elegant yet workmanlike appearance. Despite the fact that he was slightly nervous he displayed a magnificence I had never seen in a dog and I enthused on his appearance to my classmates the next Monday as we sat sipping our compulsory school milk up our equally compulsory straws.

In the right hands I have no doubt that Arno would have emulated one of those super dogs of literature – one of those larger than life type animals found in R. M. Ballantyne's books or in a short story penned by Jack London. He was large, powerful, and sagacious in appearance with the noble head of a canine super hero. He radiated intelligence and should have been trained. Indeed, I repeat, in the right hands Arno would have become an incredibly good dog; loyal, devoted and brilliantly clever. Sadly, Mr Webb's hands were certainly not the right ones as Mr Webb (and myself alas) were to discover.

I raced through my grocery round the following Saturday leaving a precious tin of salmon on the doorstep of Ricky Jones Llandovery who didn't like fish of any sort, and a packet of baby's nappies in the basket of Miss Emily Hills, a ferocious spinster lady who ruled the local girls' school and had no intention of matrimony let alone parenthood. My mistakes I confess were the result of rushing my more mundane deliveries in order to see Mr Webb and his Alsatian Arno once more.

Arno was settled in by now and had marked out the yard as his domain. As I stepped into the yard he approached me stiff-legged as though challenging me to back down and submit to him and he froze when I attempted to touch him. In short he displayed all the symptoms of a dog that was in the process of becoming what some dog psychologists refer to as an Alpha male – an animal which needed to be taken in hand and trained – and taken in hand quickly, I must add. I was twelve years old and unable to realise a metamorphosis was taking place although I suddenly became intensely suspicious of the animal. However, the rather weakly Mr Webb should have realised he was in possession of a biological time bomb. Sadly Mr Webb had neither perspicacity nor ability to control difficult dogs and was about to suffer as a result of his inadequacies.

That Monday I enthused somewhat less on the beauty and power of Mr Webb's Arno, for I had inherited the title of 'class bore' from Byron Bowen who knew the registration numbers of every car in our automobile starved valley. Furthermore, by the time I collected my box of groceries from Mr Beynon, the grocer, and had mounted the saddle of that inordinately heavy delivery bike, I had a curious sense of foreboding about delivering my 'bundle' to Mr Webb. That day I delivered carefully, meticulously carefully, taking next week's order from the reclusive Barby Jones (via the letterbox) standing almost to attention as Miss Hills, starched back with whiter than white blouse, checked her parcel and chided me about the mistakes I made the week previous and endured an absolute tirade from the fish loathing Ricky Jones of Llandovery, who for some reason had peeled the label from the side of the tin of salmon before returning the unwanted can.

It was almost as if I had some sense of misgiving about delivering Mr Webb's parcel and facing the arrogant Arno – and perhaps it was my nervousness and trepidation that helped trigger off the reaction from the beast. Whatever the reason he was alert and ready for action long before my grocer's bike creaked and groaned along the path leading to the gate and perhaps, just perhaps, he became even more hostile as a result of my piteous cries for Mr Webb. Arno stood watching me on the far side of the yard, his eyes expressionless and his somewhat lupine face alert and hostile. It would have been a mistake to open the gate, folly to step into the yard, sheer insanity to walk towards the front door, the knocker of which was shaped like the head of a ravening fiend, but I was twelve at the time – and this poor excuse is all I shall offer for provoking the frenzy that followed.

If I had expected the stealthy stalk of the wall-eyed collie, the strange ritual enacted out by this pale blue-grey dog, I was to be mistaken. Arno was on me with a rush, an attack that bore me earthwards, dashing my face against the stones and with an almost meticulous thoroughness he set about attempting to kill me. He seized my jacket and I swear he shook me from the floor as a terrier would worry a rat – and perhaps almost as effortlessly. I felt my face brush the ground several times as Arno continued to shake me and I am convinced that had I had the courage to struggle, he would have killed me.

As it was perhaps my fear, no, my stark terror, which probably saved me, for the rush of the dog, the furious impact of Alsatian meets boy and the fall which badly winded me, ensured my silence and immobility, giving the rather sickly looking Mr Webb an opportunity to haul the beast from atop of me.

Later, when I taught a class of aggressive and disturbed youths, I heard tales of how these underfed and often emaciated boys supposedly were able to kill an attacking German Shepherd Dog. Such tales are simply lies, aided and abetted by total ignorance of the power displayed by an attacking large dog. Such tales also indicate a lack of knowledge of human behaviour when the said human is under attack. The rush of a fully grown male German Shepherd Dog is easily enough to down a seasoned heavyweight boxer and once the dog is able to inflict its first crippling bite, a curious biochemical reaction takes place in the victim under attack. Lions apparently devour live zebras while the zebras display an extraordinary composure during the process and seem almost oblivious to the frightful pain they must be experiencing (incidentally the popularity of television programmes which seem to go out of their way to show such horror is, to say the least, disturbing). This inertia is simply because once flesh is torn or mutilated the body produces substances called endorphins, morphine-like substances, which tend to reduce the agony of being eaten alive. Livingstone describes his sensations after being attacked by a lion and records that he behaved like someone drugged, experiencing little pain but considerable numbness as the lion shook and attempted to kill him.

Thus a person attacked by a dog is not only terrified but also tranquillised by the body's natural anaesthetic and the quality and quantity of endorphins is greatly increased once the dog's teeth puncture tissue more deeply. It is believed by some that acupuncture eases pain simply because the tiny needles may cause the release of endorphins. Thus if tiny needles painlessly inserted into the epidermis will provoke such a reaction how much more so will the crushing, macerating bite of a large dog? Therefore even if the victim – and victim accurately describes anyone under attack by a large dog – wished to retaliate and take the battle to the attacker, he would be unable to do so.

I had been shaken like a rat by Arno, lifted from the ground by the sheer fury of the animal and my nose, which had been brushed repeatedly against the stones of the cobbled yard, continued to bleed and bleed copiously for the rest of the day. Furthermore, such was the terror I experienced, that twice I stopped pedalling the grocer's bike home and panted like an asthmatic experiencing a particularly severe attack.

I left Mr Webb's groceries outside the gate henceforth, for I was not convinced that the heavy chain which now restrained the dog, a chain with links strong enough to restrain an infuriated Cerberus, or a ravening Fenris Wolf, would prevent the enraged brute dismembering me as he lunged and seemingly screamed execrations as I approached the farmstead. It was in fact the first time I had ever been afraid of a dog and until that time I was unaware of just how dangerous a dog of any breed could be.

If I might chance my luck and risk yet another digression, the biting power of even a small dog is invariably underestimated by both the owner and the potential victim of an attack. Jack London's 'Jerry' the eponymous hero of the book *Jerry of the Islands* is an Irish terrier, a medium-sized dog with a courage 'greatly in excess of its size'. It drives off only shiftless Kanakas and sly-eyed Chinese but is kind and gentle with honest white men – London was a fearsome racist. Yet the mental image of terrified Chinese coolies and drunken Polynesians fleeing before a tiny terrier-sized dog seemed amazing even to devotees of London's books. However, Cummings, an American behaviourist with a particular interest in the behaviour of dogs cast adrift on America's streets, is convinced that a dog the size of an Irish terrier is more than capable of incapacitating and eventually killing a grown and healthy man.

I learned quite a lot about dogs during my grocery round, particularly about the behaviour of potentially hostile dogs and of the curious ritual that usually precedes an attack on a human being. Above all I learned not to run when a dog attacked me, for the meanest tiny mongrel can easily outrun a man – in 1794 a terrier ran a mile in 2 minutes thereby making an athlete of the calibre of Steve Cram appear something of a slouch. I was later to put the knowledge to good use, although the experience I am about to relate made me even more fearful of German Shepherd Dogs.

During the years 1955–1957 I experienced a hurting, damaging, dispiriting, soul destroying stint known as National Service, a two year period of drudgery and pointless degradation which convinced me that not only was I ill-equipped to be a soldier, but that I was never designed to live in a billet with thirty-two members of my own species. Thus I flouted minor rules and endured horrendous punishments as a result of my disregard for military convention.

One night, while returning late to camp, a comrade of mine suggested that we should climb the wires to get to the billet, an ill-advised move as the camp was well patrolled because of alleged IRA activity in the area. What was more foolish still was the fact that the point at which we attempted to climb the perimeter fencing was adjacent to the armoury, an area which was certain to be heavily patrolled.

We climbed the fence, negotiated the barbed wire strand by dint of throwing our capes over the wire, and slithered into the camp. Our intrusion was marked by a shout, a blaze of lights and an attack from one the camp security dogs, an ugly, longhaired, German Shepherd Dog which bore down on us at an incredible rate. I should like to be able to say that my cool, calm attitude saved the day and that I had the presence of mind to remain perfectly still. It would be a lie. I froze to immobility because I was afraid, and possibly because I am a coward by nature, I resigned myself to the fate that awaited me rather than attempting to escape the attention of the dog by dint of flight. My comrade was made of sterner stuff and attempted to run and the futility of flight before such a dog and the awesome power of a German Shepherd Dog instantly became apparent.

My friend was struck in the back by the leaping dog and borne earthwards by the force of the attack. While I, coward that I am, froze against the fence and witnessed the fearsome carnage that was enacted. The dog shook and worried my comrade as if the twelve-stone youth was a rag doll and seemingly took an unwholesome pleasure in the attack, wagging its tail as it savaged my comrade, before the handler arrived at the scene and brought an end to the havoc. Amongst the carnage being enacted, the shouting, the screaming, the furious roar of the dog and the confusion caused by sound, aided and abetted by bright lights I managed to slip away undetected. It speaks highly of my friend that he claimed to be alone and hence my misconduct was never detected, but as a result of my experience I became decidedly cautious about owning a German Shepherd Dog and never considered keeping one – well at least until I was forced into purchasing a guard dog – but once again I seem to have run ahead of my tale.

CHAPTER 1

The High Price of Fame

Until my fortieth birthday I enjoyed a life of unparalleled mediocrity. I have never been particularly bright and my career in the professional boxing ring made me acutely aware of my physical shortcomings. I ceased to box after my thirty-second birthday, by which time I was convinced that I was as ill equipped to make a living as a boxer as I was to be a teacher. I strayed from school to school accepting leaving presents, usually dictionaries for some reason or other, from heads and fellow teachers who sighed with relief at my departure. For a while I tried part-time jobs, worked spells on the motorways, delivered van loads of fish, eviscerated dead and rather bored looking turkeys and even worked as a cloakroom attendant at a dance hall which acted as a front for a slightly less legal activity. However, by no stretch of the imagination could I have been considered a success at any of these occupations. After a while I realised that I was one of those social misfits, and worse still, I began to accept the fact. From time to time I obtained some consolation from reading *Reader's Digest*-type articles which indicated that there was always light at the end of life's tunnel and there was a place in the world for virtually anyone. However, such consolation afforded me only a rather temporary lift, and in next to no time my spirits sank yet once again and I became reconciled to the fact I was destined to be a failure, one of those mute inglorious Miltons or bloodless Cromwells straight out of the pages of *Elegy In A Country Churchyard*, perhaps, but a failure nevertheless. At one time it seemed that everything to which I turned my hand was doomed to failure. During my thirty-something period my spirits sank to an all-time low due to constant conflict with various headmasters under which I was forced to serve, and at times I envied the cadavers of squashed motorway rabbits which at least were spared the torture of life's trials and tribulations.

During my fortieth year, however, my luck changed – although at times I questioned whether it was for the better or the worse. In a moment of idleness I penned my first book, a slim volume called *Tales of a Rat Hunting Man,* which I began somewhat tentatively, but as the text progressed, I wrote with almost manic enthusiasm and completed in something slightly in excess of forty-eight furious hours. Curiously my three days of sleeplessness left me feeling exhilarated rather than exhausted and I glowed with pride at the sight of the two Jumbo Jotters that contained the manuscript of the book. On reflection, coloured by the fact that *Rat Hunting Man* was penned some forty books ago, the book seems trite, decidedly amateurish and badly crafted. Yet it was an exhilarating book to write and started me off on a career as a writer – well a writer of sorts. My fortieth year was tumultuous by any standards. After the publication of a hastily written book called *Modern Ferreting* I was favoured by a monumental piece of good luck, although I confess the occasion did not seem quite as fortuitous at the time. Ferrets were at that time considered to be somewhat mysterious animals, and ferreters, or those who owned ferrets, were expected to look and act like Lil Abner type rustics, hot foot out of the 'hookworm belt'. I confess I looked the part. My clothes had always had that uncared for look and my hair has resisted the efforts of barbers and combs to shape it. I have always had that scruffy look even when favoured by a new suit, indeed I once boasted the appellation 'The Sultan of Shabbiness', and hence when I was asked to appear on a television show to publicise my book *Modern Ferreting* I must have appeared an interviewer's dream – a rustic, peculiar, unkempt eccentric who kept and worked ferrets. Ferrets, so the interviewer believed, were funny creatures, humorous beasts – but the resulting interview perhaps proved just how unfunny or unhumourous a ferret could be – depending on which side of the camera the observer was standing of course.

The show was Yorkshire Television's 'Calendar' and the victim chosen to conduct the interview Richard Whitely, who at the time of writing, hosts that intellectual's game show 'Countdown' – which consists of compiling words from jumbles of letters, unravelling anagrams and solving mathematical problems designed to confound a latterday Isaac Newton. Indeed the show is a far cry from interviewing an untidy rustic with a bag of ferrets!

The interview was scheduled to be a supporting feature for a chat with ventriloquist Roger De Coursey who performed with an impertinent Teddy Bear called Nookie – a toy with amazingly expressive eyes and a rather foul mouth. However, while De Coursey handled his interview with aplomb and panache expected of a seasoned performer, my own interview went horribly wrong.

To cut a very long story somewhat short, I had borrowed some white ferrets from a rather unreliable friend and the ferrets were unusually silly rather than nasty. Whitely, rather courageously and slightly nonchalantly, handled the ferrets for several minutes before the interview began and given confidence by the kitten-like tameness of the ferrets, really took liberties with the creatures during the interview. Quite suddenly one of the ferrets playfully seized one of Whitely's fingers and held it. Now, I say 'playfully' because an angry, frightened ferret bites with great fury and punctures human flesh as easily as would the needle of a hypodermic syringe. The young ferret bit playfully but hung on, gripping Whitely's finger a shade too enthusiastically perhaps. The interview went out live and was terminated at this point although the incident caused great hilarity amongst the camera team.

I drove home from Leeds to my house in Lichfield a shade dispirited by the events of the day, and my embarrassment was exacerbated by the fact that friends living in the Yorkshire area telephoned me to say how much they had enjoyed the bedlam they had witnessed. If I ever cherished aspirations about enjoying a career in television, and I confess I never did, my hopes of further television work were dashed asunder by the events of the day. Or so I thought.

I had almost forgotten the Yorkshire Television debacle and had sunk back into my banal teaching life when yet another company, London Weekend Television, telephoned and asked my permission to use the clip of Whitely v Ferret for a show hosted by Dennis Norden and called 'It'll Be Alright On The Night' – a compendium of clips of other interviews which had gone slightly awry. I will terminate my tale by saying the foul-up at Yorkshire Television became one of the most repeated clips on television and was shown in numerous countries throughout the world.

A host of television and radio interviews followed, and BBC2 and Yorkshire Television then made two documentaries concerning my weird and erratic lifestyle. Newspapers also sent reporters to interview me and most seemed to require me to show them ferrets and for some curious reason, handle live rats; for seemingly the British public have a penchant for the repellent and rats represent the most repellent of beasts to the man in the street. Fame is indeed quite a heady drug and I confess I quite enjoyed my brief spell of notoriety. However, fame like most drugs has unpleasant side effects.

My programmes attracted the attention of some rather questionable people from Walsall and forthwith my life took on the nature of a living Hell. At first only my terriers were stolen, and the police obtained two convictions against the culprits. However, as time advanced, my torturers became more bold and invaded property, looting all the pitiful valuables I had acquired during my lifetime, stealing even the money box I set aside to fill with change and donate to certain charities. God knows, I had little property worth stealing, but what I had my burglars stole.

What was worse, each time my house was ransacked – and I was burgled a total of eighty three times – the property the thieves had handled but refrained from taking, felt dirty and soiled. Once my house was left decidedly filthy after a raid, for my thieves fouled on one of the rugs and trampled in their ordure. I felt horribly sick after the incident and stayed the night with a friend, only to return the following morning to find my torturers had returned during the night and taken some of the goods they had overlooked during the daytime raid. A police sergeant simply told me that living in a house so remote simply invited the attentions of felons, but such simple homespun and easily imparted logic offered little solace and the raids on my property continued to be perpetrated.

It would be wrong to assume I am naturally antipathetic to the police. Indeed I believe that the police force stands between the public and out and out anarchy. However, I don't believe that some officers try particularly hard to arrest criminals and I believe the rest of the public probably share my feelings. Neighbourhood watches and groups more akin to vigilantes are sprouting up around the countryside to compensate for the inadequacies of the police as a whole. I confess a policeman's life isn't a happy one, perhaps, but I do feel that some of the CID officers don't try as hard as they might.

When my house was pillaged I fitted bigger locks as the police advised. My burglars then kicked in the ornamental panels on the doors and entered via the holes in the damaged woodwork. When my windows were smashed, I covered the windows with heavy gauge concrete reinforced wire, but the havoc continued until I fitted the windows with heavy wooden shutters. This too did little to deter my burglars and the cry of 'Fit bigger locks' from the CID did little to help my despair. My house resembled the hidey-hole of the Prisoner of Zenda but still the raids continued and I began to dread returning home at night lest I found that yet once again my premises had been invaded. Life became a living Hell.

I obtained a temporary respite from the raids after my car was mutilated by someone who poured paint stripper over the bonnet and the press began to take notice of my plight. One newspaper published the number of undetected burglaries that had been perpetrated on my home but this caused even more trouble. A senior police officer telephoned the school where I taught and demanded an interview in a talk 'loud and quickly' voice, speaking in a staccato manner resonating the sound in the buccal cavity, adopted by officers who are nonplussed about what to do. I declined the interview, wrote to my MP, and the officer's threat of prosecuting me for complaining about police incompetence never came to fruition.

At this point in the saga I became the subject of an insurance investigation for the insurance company I had used for years was obviously perplexed by my constant claims for damaged and stolen goods. I was investigated by a young and meticulous insurance officer who saw the damage perpetrated by thieves and, thank God, substantiated my claims. However, so frequent were the raids that the insurance company refused to insure me, and so for that matter did every other insurance company I contacted. I felt desperate and, frankly, naked and vulnerable.

At this point in the tale my friend Eddie Judd, an RAF police dog handler, entered the saga and suggested that in addition to the Fort Knox type security measures I had adopted, I should invest in guard dogs, and here, dear reader, begins the tale proper so to speak. I constantly send up a prayer to Eddie for intervening when he did. Without him I would have lost the little sanity I still possess – and without him I wouldn't have bought Polly.

However, before proceeding it is expedient to discuss the subject of guard dogs and at the time of writing this is a hot potato.

CHAPTER 2

Guard Dogs

I'm not sure I like the American attitude towards life and property; perhaps I should explain that comment fairly quickly. A few weeks ago, a Scot knocked on the door of some house in the USA, and was shot dead for his trespass. Such behaviour would be unthinkable in Britain. What disturbs me more, however, is the tale of a commercial traveller who was killed and damn nigh eaten by a ban dog (and I'll explain the term later) after the unsuspecting salesman had walked into a house to peddle his wares. I know double-glazing salesmen can be particularly annoying at times – and cavity insulation promoters can be almost as annoying – no one but no one in Britain would read of this type of atrocity and think, 'Serve the beggar right for walking into peoples' homes uninvited'. Come to think of it though, it would lend a new twist to the plot of *Death of a Salesman*!

The British way of life, and I don't apologise for such a pompous sounding statement, dictates that natives of our islands must value life more than property. Hence, while one may feel it just or reasonable to have one's guard dog dismember a burglar who breaks into one's house, both the police and the Director of Public Prosecutions may take a somewhat different view of the subject. Likewise, shooting a burglar is somewhat frowned upon in Britain, as a recent controversial case indicates.

There are in fact rather severe restrictions on the ownership of a savage guard dog particularly if the dog is required to guard business premises. During the late 1960s and early 1970s there was a spate of attacks perpetrated by guard dogs chained to posts and rails in order that they might guard scrap yards and industrial premises, and the bête noire of dogdom was at that time the German Shepherd Dog, a breed the media falsely accused of being treacherous and totally untrustworthy and, because of this, at that time it was almost impossible to sell even good German Shepherd Dog puppies. So publicised were the attacks of these monstrous guard dogs, that the government were pressured into passing the Guard Dog Act of 1975, which insists that unless a dog is used to guard or protect agricultural land or dwelling houses it is an offence to keep a dog specifically trained to be a guard unless that dog is accompanied by a handler and if the handler is not present the dog must be secured (locked in a secure building?) and not allowed to roam freely around the premises, a regulation that rather defeats the purpose of keeping a guard dog perhaps, but then Britain's laws suggest that we place a higher price on life than on property.

In fact, while one High Court Judge decreed that there was little point in keeping a guard dog unless the dog had the disposition to be a guard, i.e. was hostile to unwanted intruders, it is fair to say that in Britain at least, a guard dog should deter rather than mangle or mutilate intruders, and the thought of being killed and partly eaten by an American ban dog still beggars thinking about. American ban dogs are bred by crossing certain strains of pit bull terrier with Neapolitan mastiffs to create a ferocious man-biting guard dog whose movements are restricted by chains, hence banded or chained dogs. The strains of pit bull terrier used in the creation of these monstrous brutes have to be chosen with care, for despite the regulations imposed by the 1992 Dangerous Dogs Act, few pit bull terriers are man-haters and most tolerate the attention of small children with great patience. Incidentally, the ban dogs of Arthurian legend and Coleridge-type poems were usually mastiffs or large dogs of unknown breeds. The very presence of a guard dog, the actual appearance of the animal, should in fact be enough to deter someone who is considering breaking into one's premises.

Now, it is a curious fact that the size of a dog alone seldom frightens a would-be burglar. A St. Bernard is easily capable of killing a man (so is an Irish terrier sized dog if Cummings is correct) but the presence of a St. Bernard is seldom enough to deter an enthusiastic burglar. In fact there is some evidence to suggest that the St. Bernard, which incidentally is a type of mastiff and has an awesome bite, have been deliberately bred to have a benign appearance simply because of the type of work it was bred to do. Such a dog was bred to seek out travellers trapped in the snows near the St. Bernard monastery and the sight of a fearsome looking dog, whether or not it was carrying a keg of obligatory life-giving brandy, was likely to exacerbate the state of shock from which the traveller was suffering rather that give the wretched person an element of confidence that help was at hand. Subsequently, this giant mastiff was deliberately, or perhaps unintentionally, bred to have a benign, gentle appearance, to allay the fears of travellers buried in the snow (or so Brockendon, *Illustrations of the Passes of the Alps* (1828), believed). This, despite the fact that an enraged St. Bernard can be a devil incarnate.

So what exactly does deter a burglar from entering one's premises or that relatively new breed of criminal, the mugger, who was once simply known as a footpad, from attacking a pedestrian or breaking into a car to attack a woman? Well, firstly Cummings, who researched people's attitudes to dogs, found that dark coloured or dark faced dogs had a greater deterrent value that dogs which were lighter coloured or white. Hence, the three great deterrent, or guard, dogs the Dobermann, the Rottweiler and the German Shepherd Dog are usually black and tan in colour and have dark, and therefore more menacing, faces. Likewise, bullmastiffs, which are usually a soft, attractive fawn colour or red (good brindle mastiffs are rare) are bred with black masks possibly because this mask acts as a sematic, or warning, marking and deters hostile intruders.

The publicity afforded by the media also colours the public's opinion of how dangerous certain breeds of dog actually are. Prior to the 1975 Act most newspapers suggested that the German Shepherd Dog was the dog to fear and there were moves afoot to attempt to prohibit the keeping of them. In fact, if it were not for the sterling work the German Shepherd Dog did as guide dogs for the blind, hearing dogs for the deaf and search-and-rescue dogs in deep snow or the rubble of bombed out buildings, I feel that one of the more extreme pressure groups, which seem to hold sway over both common-sense and central government, would have successfully lobbied parliament to introduce a bill outlawing the German Shepherd Dog and perhaps pre-empting the 1992 Dangerous Dogs Act by two decades or more.

However, it was not the 1975 Guard Dog Act which gave the Dobermann and the Rottweiler the fearsome reputation they were to enjoy for the next fifteen years or so but two films both of which, curiously enough, starred Gregory Peck.

In 1976 Peck produced and starred in the horror film *The Omen* – a rather terrifying piece of hokum which concerns a man who finds his child is the spawn of the devil, desperately and rather pointlessly evil, with the obligatory 666 mark as suggested in *Revelations*. Peck realising his child is a monstrous changeling attempts to abduct and kill the infant who is protected by a rather small but totally hostile Rottweiler, which attempts to tear Peck limb from limb in its efforts to protect the satanic child.

Within weeks of the release of the film unscrupulous breeders of Rottweilers were advertising puppies as 'Devil Dogs' or 'Damien Dogs' as seen in the film *The Omen*. The outcome of this publicity was, alas, far reaching, for the sort of person who would be influenced by such a film and induced to buy a guard dog of the sort that nearly 'saw off' poor Gregory, would be not only mentally immature but a person (usually a man) who enjoyed a very low level of self-esteem. Hence the purchase of a puppy by such a person produced a very undesirable and decidedly unstable partnership – an epsilon type person owned by an Alpha category dog – for some Rottweilers are very strong willed and require careful handling if they are not to grow into biological time bombs. In the right hands a Rottweiler is a delightful animal, quick to learn, easy to train and responsive to firm but not harsh discipline. In the hands of a weak man, a man who seeks to elevate himself in the eyes of his fellow human beings by the ownership of a large potentially dangerous dog, a Rottweiler, particularly a dominant male Rottweiler, becomes a lethal weapon.

Within two years of the release of *The Omen* reports of attacks by Rottweilers on small children and adults alike began to flood in and the media obtained much copy from these horrific events. In 1987 in fact, a sick comedian appeared in one of the northern working men's clubs and was pilloried because of an unfunny wisecrack, 'What has four legs and a baby's head? – A Rottweiler!' – a hideous faux pas as it happened, for the most recent attack by a Rottweiler had been perpetrated in a village near the club. However, this train of events firmly established the Rottweiler as the dog to fear.

Likewise the Dobermann shot to prominence as a guard dog shortly after the release of *The Boys From Brazil* – a well-written, if somewhat barmy book by Ira Levin – and the film was equally absurd, one must add. Briefly, the gist of the plot is that shortly before Hitler died in the bunker in Berlin suicide pact, he allowed a doctor to scrape samples of skin and flesh from his back and chest. These were preserved and clones produced from the Hitler cells – young blond youths with smug, self-satisfied faces and a total disregard for human suffering. Peck, who plays the insanely sadistic Dr Mengele, who nurtured the embryonic clones, has to ensure that not only is the gene structure of the future Führer exact but the traumas of the infant Hitler's life also replicated, kills one of the clone's fathers who just happens to breed Dobermanns. In turn the Dobermanns, on the instigation of one of the clones, literally tear Peck (who seems singularly prone to attacks from large canines) to pieces and the last scenes of the film are, to say the least, horrific.

Now in point of fact, Peck gave an interview concerning the film and describes the dogs which attack him as 'pussy cats' which were not the slightest bit hostile to either Peck or the camera crew. The attack was staged simply by attaching objects to Peck's sleeves and lapels and then the dogs were told to 'fetch' the said objects. This is a particularly common way of training film dogs to feign an attack on a human being and was perfected by one of the stunt men who worked alongside Mack Sennet, although in one such scene, the feigned attack on a man went terribly wrong. The screams and snarls were added to the soundtrack at a later stage and Peck confessed he had to suppress laughter as the dogs attempted to lick his face as the sequence progressed.

Yet immediately after the film was released, breeders of Dobermanns were besieged by would-be buyers wishing to purchase Dobermanns for all the wrong reasons. The film *The Dobermann Gang*, a cleverly staged piece of nonsense about a team of Dobermanns taught to rob a bank more in the Disney rather than Hitchcock vein, failed to interest the dog buying public but each repeat of *The Boys From Brazil* brings a spate of would-be half-crazy potential dog purchasing clients out of the woodwork.

However, the Dobermann received yet another shot in the arm in the popularity stakes, at least as far as the emotionally disturbed punter is concerned. During the same decade the Colombo series featured the famous *Dial For Murder* 'Rosebud' incident, quite a well-staged production in which a behaviourist played by Nicol Williamson trained a a pair of Dobermanns to attack and kill when someone utters the word 'Rosebud'. Now as this word is seldom used in conversation the dogs remain almost inert in the company of their would-be victim. Until, that is, the behaviourist phones his victim and asks the name of the sled in the film *Citizen Kane*. The victim utters 'Rosebud' while speaking on the telephone and this triggers the two Dobermanns to perpetrate the most horrendous attack on the victim, who dies as a result of the furious mauling he receives.

Each time this episode is shown, Dobermann breeders are inundated with requests to supply puppies capable of emulating the feats of the two Dobermanns in the programme, although how such people manage to dial while restricted by the cosy confines of their straight-jackets is rather puzzling!

Now the Rosebud sequence is not quite as farfetched as the layman dog owner may suspect, and it is simplicity itself to train a dog to certain words or gestures. The Punchinello type circus dogs, the scruffy mongrel performing amongst the beautifully groomed poodles, performing every trick badly while the poodles behave impeccably, is usually trained to react only to certain gestures from the handler. Of course such animals are superbly trained and as a valediction to the act, so to speak, perform each trick impeccably. This change of heart or attitude is usually wrought by the handler clicking her fingernails to cause the dog to perform wrongly and then neglecting to perform this act when she wishes the dog to perform well.

On a more relevant if more sinister note, security dogs used for crowd control at football matches or protest meetings are conditioned to react to certain words from members of the crowd. As the abusive expletive 'Bastard' usually precedes any attack, crowd control dogs are sometimes trained to bite or bark fiercely when any member of the crowd acts in a menacing way and utters this word.

Now personally, should I possess both the inclination and the energy to consider burglary as a profession, I would stay well clear of any household which kept a bullmastiff, as some of these dogs, particularly if restricted by a chain, can be unholy terrors. This breed is simply a hybrid form of the larger mastiff type and the degenerate mastiff, or as it was known from 1632 onwards, the bulldog. After the anti-poaching acts of the 1830s gave almost limitless power to gamekeepers and landowners alike, there was a great market for dogs that would face down an armed poacher and hence gamekeepers' night dogs or bullmastiffs were developed. Some of these beasts were fearsome animals and became even more fearsome when restricted by a chain.

On the subject of terror it is expedient perhaps to mention the bullmastiff Thorneywood Terror, bred by a Mr Burton of Thorneywood, Nottingham. In 1910 *The Field* reported that Mr Burton showed his dog Thorneywood Terror and offered a pound (a week's wages for a farm worker at that time) to any man who could escape the dog even though the dog was securely muzzled. One man volunteered to act as the 'runner' and was given a long start before the dog was slipped at him but was pinned and knocked nearly senseless by the muzzled beast. One can only imagine the fate of the victim of the dog had managed to slip its muzzle.

Mastiff types become fearsomely protective of territory if their movements are restricted by chains – hence the word ban dog or banded or chained dog. In the late 1980s there was a craze to produce these ferocious animals and to recreate the awesome mastiffs of yesteryear. In

Britain and America this was done by mating more phlegmatic types of mastiff with American pit bull terriers and the resulting hybrids often possessed the power and strength of the mastiff and the furious tenacity of the American pit bull terrier. The breeding of these ban dogs would have been big business in Britain had not the breeding programme been rather fortunately curtailed by the Dangerous Dogs Act of 1992, which forbid the breeding of pit bull terriers and hybrid forms of these animals.

The bite of any mastiff is quite terrifyingly powerful and such a statement literally begs a tale. In July 1997 a young child was eating an ice cream when an apparently innocuous bullmastiff attempted to seize the cone. In doing so, the bullmastiff not only bit off but swallowed the child's lip. The tale becomes even more amazing for while the child was rushed to hospital the bullmastiff was put to death and the lip extracted from its stomach. A surgeon then grafted the lip on the child and apparently the graft was successful. A quarter of a century ago such a tale would have been the stuff of science fiction.

However, the most obviously protective of dogs, the most suitable dogs to keep for guard work is the common or garden German Shepherd Dog. Most police forces or security firms employ these dogs and while the majority of police forces have trained and used other breeds of dog; the Metropolitan Police Force once used Labrador retrievers, the Hong Kong Police Force boxers (which legend suggests tended to bite at the felons' genitals bringing more than just a tear to the caitiffs' eyes), Tokyo police the Akita, a giant spitz-tailed chow chow-like dog, the Federal Bureau of Investigation the Dobermann, it was only a matter of time before these agencies returned to using the more commonplace German Shepherd Dog, which is not only more readily available but far more versatile and reliable. Indeed, the breed was so obviously the best dog to guard one's house that it is all the more amazing that I bought a Dobermann, or to be a shade more precise, a pair of Dobermanns, as guards and from thenceforth the nightmare really began.

CHAPTER 3

The Dobermanns

I feel a shade hypocritical when I write advising people on the correct dog to purchase, particularly when I suggest the reader ignores the eulogies found in the breed books. Such breed books are usually written by enthusiasts who are besotted with specific breeds and are blind to the obvious faults such breeds are known to possess. For instance, there was uproar recently from the Golden Retriever Clubs when Dr Mugford suggested that certain strains of retriever were prone to produce animals which manifested a peculiarity similar to cocker rage. Yet Mugford, while not a favourite writer of mine, is a meticulous researcher who would not have published his findings unless he was absolutely certain of the facts. If the Yiddish proverb 'No fishmonger has ever been known to cry 'My fish is stinking' as a sales gimmick' is correct, likewise no breed book writer is likely to write adversely about his or her particular breed.

For instance, few Afghan hound writers are likely to state that the breed is virtually brain-dead. In fact, Glover writing in the book *Coursing* suggests Afghan hounds are too intelligent to heed the commands of their stupid human owners! Newfoundland breed books seldom mention that these giant, statuesque dogs are plagued with heart weakness and crippling hip dysplasia. Irish wolfhound breed books invariably fail to report that this huge breed of dog is short-lived and is prone to a variety of canine disorders. Likewise, I would be willing to wager that then next writer to pen about that cute little dog the West Highland white terrier is unlikely to mention the recently published veterinary paper which suggest that the breed is cursed with more genetic disorders than virtually any other breed. Indeed few fishmongers are wont to cry 'Stinking fish!'

Therefore I feel something of a fool when I not only bought a book about the Dobermann, heeded the eulogies contained therein but bought not only one but a pair of these dogs. At this point in the tale it is expedient to explain a little about the breed and why I disregarded Eddie Judd's advice and bought a pair of Dobermanns rather that German Shepherd Dogs as guard dogs.

It appears that a rent collector living in Apolda and called Louis Dobermann worked a particularly dangerous rent collecting round in the seedier districts of the town. As the rent collector was also warden of the local dog pound Dobermann had ample opportunity to acquire dogs which would be useful as protection dogs to accompany him during his rounds. Now it is a curious fact but street curs allowed to breed indiscriminately will revert to the typical black and tan colouring of the German Shepherd Dog, the Rottweiler or the Dobermann or to those red-fawn dingo-like dogs which are so numerous around council estates throughout this country. I say it is a curious fact, for if Darwin and Haekel are correct, a lengthy indiscriminate breeding programme would cause these dogs to revert to wolf-coloured stock, for wolves are supposedly (at least according to Fiennes and Fiennes) the wild ancestors of domesticated dogs. I suspect Darwin and Haekel are correct and the Fiennes are not, but I am starting to digress again.

Dobermann acquired a black and tan pedigree-unknown bitch called Schnupp which became the prototype if not the ancestor of the modern Dobermann, although breeders later modified and streamlined the breed by introducing Manchester terrier blood. The result was that the Dobermann developed into an attractive, agile dog, which had pronounced guarding instincts and jaws like steel traps. The early Dobermanns were fearsome creatures, or so tales tell, and if not ruled with an iron hand became rather recalcitrant and dangerous. Alistair MacLean in his book *The Final Frontier* tells of a spy who is cornered by the Russian secret police and seeks refuge in a tall tree. As he waits he meditates on how he will escape and on hearing the sound of tracker dogs, which he assumes are German Shepherd Dogs, he decides to fight it out with the animals and make his escape.

However, on discovering his pursuers are using Dobermanns, he decides to throw in his hand, for while he believes he can easily overcome a German Shepherd Dog he realises that he would have no chance against a Dobermann. What delicious bunkum. What outrageous hooey. I can safely assume that adroit author as he is Alistair MacLean has never witnessed an attack by a large dog of any breed, for I know of no person who is capable of withstanding an attack from even a small bitch German

Shepherd Dog. However, having said this I feel even more foolish for I believe I was influenced by MacLean's novel, which perhaps did encourage me to buy a pair of Dobermanns rather than plump for a straightforward, common or garden German Shepherd Dog. Anyway, my choice was a disastrous mistake, which turned my somewhat disorderly and troubled lifestyle into a living nightmare and here once again begins the tale proper.

I have never been particularly flush for money, a magnificent understatement for, during my years as a teacher, I lived in a state of near penury. If I wanted some minor luxury, some extra something for the cottage I was building, I took extra jobs working as a labourer, a fish deliveryman and a coal man. I hated my labouring jobs, arrived home exhausted late every evening and experienced little pleasure out of life. Yet when my home was in jeopardy and the insurance company refused to insure me once more I returned to supplementing my teaching salary with labouring jobs, to get the £500 I needed to purchase the two Dobermanns I believed I needed to guard my property.

Each evening immediately after school I returned home, fed my dogs and set out to perform my other job working as a plasterer's labourer, toiling and moiling for two plasterers who were also desperately in need of extra money. One wished to buy a holiday cottage in Devon and the other, who had bounced in and out of three marriages, had produced enough children to make potential future inbreeding a serious problem in and around Lichfield. Fecund as a granary rat, he still had sufficient energy to make my labouring job a torture supplying him with plaster that was either too dry or too fluid for his needs. On reflection, if the great inquisitor Torquemada had wished to extract a confession from a very recalcitrant heretic he could have done little better than to subject the poor wretch to a spell of labouring for two lusty and impatient plasterers. Nevertheless, I endured my torture without complaint and in silence and in eight weeks had accumulated enough money to buy my two monstrous Dobermanns, although I confess my flagging enthusiasm for the odious task of labouring was given a shot in the arm by another burglary and a police officer who investigated the break-in, a look of total indifference on his pale face and who somewhat petulantly uttered, 'We are sick of you being burgled.'

My Dobermanns were enormous and impressive. The outsized male measured thirty inches to the shoulder and weighed over one hundred and thirty pounds, while the chocolate bitch, also outsized, would also have deterred even the most determined and foolhardy of burglars, and I suppose that for a while at least, deter burglars, the pair did. However, I have a notion that the fact that one of the Midland newspapers wrote a feature on my predicament and the police's apparent indifference to my plight had something to do with keeping my torturers at bay, although the article didn't endear me to our local police force, one supposes.

I installed the Dobermanns on a Friday night and stayed with them constantly until I considered they had settled in well enough to leave them alone while I went to school to teach. They were scarcely the most restful of dogs and paced constantly along the corridor between bedrooms and living rooms, ever vigilant and seemingly never resting. When the mailman dropped circulars and bills through my letterbox on the Saturday morning the pair went berserk, terrifying the postman and attacking my ornamental front door with an unholy gusto.

I confess I watched with some satisfaction as the terrified postman leaped back to his van, screaming something unspeakable as he did so, and drove off like a stunt man from the *Dukes Of Hazzard* series. A warming glow suffused my body and I experienced a sense of security I had not felt for two or three years. My euphoria was short-lived however, for Eddie Judd arrived later that day bringing with him his almost irritating aura of pure logic.

Eddie tapped upon the front door, stepped back as the two dogs struck the woodwork with an ear-shattering crash and waited until I restrained the beasts. He eyed both a shade hypercritically before evaluating their qualities. Finally he spoke with the deliberate logic which was part and parcel of his mental make-up. 'Fine – and no one is likely to break into your house,' he said. 'All that will happen now is that the thieves will loot your kennels and take every puppy you breed. Frankly,' he continued, 'I'd be amazed to see the plan you devise to keep these two in order and prevent them from killing your terriers.' My terrier pack was, incidentally, the source of great interest to my thieves and were hostile enough to attack any dog, large or small, that came near to them.

Eddie continued, 'It's not as if you can let them wander around the place. They don't know the area, would probably wander off and like as not,' he eyed the pair ominously, 'they're probably not steady with sheep.' I closed my eyes and I groaned as I imagined the havoc the pair would create if they encountered a flock of the local sheep.

'It's almost a pity that you need the pair so urgently,' Eddie explained, 'A bitch German Shepherd Dog puppy reared on the premises, allowed to wander around the cottage would be the best of guards – and,' he added a shade more ominously, 'a damned sight easier to live with than one of these.' He gasped slightly as the huge male Dobermann brushed against him, pressing him to the wall. Eddie had been a police dog handler in the RAF and believed the German Shepherd Dog to be the only suitable all-round guard dog for the average householder. He had some reservations about the tractability and courage of the Dobermann, despite the reputation the breed enjoyed and had an unfortunate experience when his own Rottweiler killed his terrier.

Eddie told amazing tales about the perspicacity of the German Shepherd Dogs he had trained while in the RAF and while he was aware of the stopping power and the intimidation of a large male German Shepherd Dog, Eddie was convinced that a bitch was a better prospect and a damn sight easier to live with. He believed that a large German Shepherd Dog male would easily overpower and possibly kill a fully-grown man and that there were few people who could overcome a determined bitch that was protective of persons and property.

'Still, you've bought these and are stuck with them,' – he nodded once more at the huge dog which was restlessly pacing the corridor followed by the chocolate bitch which was performing similarly, though perhaps a shade more quietly. 'Restful sods ain't they,' sniffed Eddie and he winked, slipping out of the front door as nimbly as a ballet dancer to avoid the rush of the huge male, who was as resentful of a person leaving the house as he was of a stranger or friend entering the premises.

I sat at home and watched television that night, although one needed the reflexes of a Bruce Lee to be able to follow the plot of a film on my flickering black and white screen. However, the exercise would perhaps allow the dogs to settle down a little, but they continued to pace up and down the corridor and bark frantically at any strange sound they heard.

I retired at midnight, my two guards still exploring the house, and slept a fitful dream-filled sleep, experiencing the sort of dreams that indicated that I was perhaps in serious need of even more serious medical treatment. In my dream I had gone to teach in a large Catholic school and while the rest of the school was attending mass, I was sent in search of a very disruptive class of children who were swimming in a deep, rubbish-filled river, diving and cavorting like happy dolphins amongst tangles of old prams and washing machines, totally ignoring my commands and pleas to leave the water. What was worse was that a huge twelve-foot white rabbit, a leftover from the 1951 Jimmy Stewart film *Harvey* raced up and own the riverbank urging my delinquent divers to ignore me. I had several of these bizarre dreams and recorded them in my diary each morning before leaving for school. It was a cathartic exercise, for at one time I used to relate these dreams to friends until I realised they were giving me strange looks and after a while ceased to come around to talk to me. However, I awoke unrefreshed and sore, only to find the two dogs were still pacing the passageway. I sat on the edge of my bed and groaned but I had little time to reflect on my situation for I was woken from my reverie by the sound of the milkman's float pulling up in the lane, the tinkle of milk bottles and the cacophonous crash of the two Dobermanns leaping at the door. I smiled smugly. No one but no one could gain entry to my home while these dogs paced inside the premises. I felt self-satisfied at my purchase and, naked as a jay bird, strode to the kitchen and switched on the kettle, and then noticed that I had used the last of the milk the previous night.

Still naked, not a pretty sight I confess, I strode to the front door and stepped into the porch to reach for the milk. It was a foolish, or perhaps an irrational, move but the seclusion of my home, the fact that the premises were far off the beaten track, had allowed me to forget natural modesty. However I had reckoned without the giant Dobermann male and his dislike for anyone entering or leaving the premises. As he watched my naked torso creep into the porch he rushed, slamming the door behind me, leaving me standing, milk bottle in hand, in the porch.

The lane adjacent to my cottage was seldom used by traffic, or pedestrians for that matter – at least that was what I believed before that fateful day in autumn when I found myself locked out of the house, naked as the day I was born, in a porch constructed largely of all too transparent glass. I stood there shivering while engaging in a rather futile attempt at gaining entry to the house, while the Dobermann leaped against the door roaring menaces at the naked denizen of the porch.

However, after a while my panic abated somewhat and I resolved to wait for a suitable moment, run naked into the lane, through the nettle filled garden and force an entry via my kitchen window. However, to maltreat a proverb so to speak, 'There is many a slip twixt porch and kitchen window'.

I steeled myself for my naked dash, steadying myself to rush buck naked into the road and run the twelve yards to the sanctuary of my garden, when the sound of a motor vehicle dissuaded me from my course of action. I flung myself to the floor of the porch, pressing my body to the freezing concrete, hoping to be overlooked by the occupants of the passing car. After what seemed an eternity the car trickled past my house and down the lane and I prepared yet again to make the mad dash to the sanctuary of my nettle filled garden. Quite suddenly yet another sound alerted me to the approach of yet another motor vehicle, so once again I pressed myself to the concrete floor, hoping and praying the vehicle would not stop at my cottage.

Once more the car drove slowly past my cottage with what I surmised to be a middle-aged couple commenting on the huge growth of goat beard, or wild clematis, which had started to cover my windows. I glanced at my watch, the only item I possessed with which I could possibly cover my modesty, and realised that it was nearly midday and I had stood, and lain, in that freezing porch for nearly an hour.

I attempted a half-crouch, steeling myself to make the short dash through the nettle bed and force and entry through the kitchen window while the two dogs continued to bay frantically from the sanctuary of the house, eager to hurt, maim or kill the naked person crouching in a sinister posture in the porch.

The cacophonous baying ceased awhile, allowing the brutes to regain their breath perhaps and once more I prepared to make my dash. To my horror, during a lull in the barking, I heard the sound of a troupe of children walking along the road and, peeping over the top of the brick built base of the porch, I spied a troupe of Brownies dancing along the lane accompanied by one of the sundry 'owls' who are wont to accompany Brownies. Once more I flattened myself to the floor and listened in horror as the troupe strode by singing a song which was a familiar army refrain, though the words of the ditty were somewhat different from the ones I learned at Aldershot! Chilled to the bone, cursing the Baden-Powells, and 'owls' in general, I let the troupe pass and, throwing caution to the wind, made my mad dash into the road, round the back of the house, through the nettle beds, smashing the kitchen window, prising back the metal bars I had constructed as burglar deterrents and climbing into the house via the kitchen sink. All the while my Dobermanns pounded the kitchen door as though desperate to tear asunder the naked intruder who had the temerity to break through the kitchen window.

I sat swathed in towels to prevent hypothermia until the barking had quietened to a frenzied roaring and contemplated how the media would have treated the tale if one of the stragglers of the Brownie troupe had chanced upon the streaker making his dash along the road. 'Should This Monster Be Allowed To Teach Our Children?' was the most tame and kindliest of headlines I could imagine and I winced at the way *Private Eye* might have treated the tale had I been observed.

When I had calmed the guard dogs sufficiently for me to leave the kitchen and dress I telephoned Eddie, who, despite my obvious distress and indignation, roared with laughter at the tale while I suffered the

tortures of the damned trying to ease the effects of nettles on naked and very private skin, while my flesh developed a rash reminiscent of something out of the *Quatermass* experiment. 'A bitch German Shepherd Dog puppy would have prevented all this nonsense,' he commented shortly before he rang off, but then Eddie's answer to any problem, his only panacea, seemed to be the purchase of a German Shepherd Dog bitch puppy.

The following Sunday was an unbearable Hell. Whittington, once a quiet country village when I first moved to the district, had become a dormitory town for Birmingham, peopled with middle class, first-house buying young executives, none of whom had the slightest idea of life in a country village, but all of whom were hell-bent on creating a mythical Erewhon, a typical country village. At one time during the early stages of the executive invasion certain members of the new community attempted to publish a broadsheet called 'Whittingfun'. I was approached by a very genial lady driving a smart new red Volvo and asked if I minded being the 'fun' of the 'Whittingfun' broadsheet, for at that time my house was virtually a ruin and almost an embarrassment to the district. I was at a particularly low level of my life at that time, when job prospects were almost zero and my future looked decidedly grim, so I declined the opportunity to be lampooned in 'Whittingfun' – no matter how harmless the 'fun' might be.

What were more maddening, were the infernal treasure hunts, however, and for those who are not conversant with these activities, perhaps I'd best explain. Treasure hunts are harmless pursuits and consist of groups of car-driving people driving around the district following a route dictated by a series of obscure clues, each clue having to be solved before the group sought out the next object or landmark – and alas my cottage had become a conspicuous landmark in the district around Whittington. I had no training as a builder when I purchased a set of second-hand rafters and started to construct the roof of my cottage, hence ineptitude and a gravitational phenomenon known as 'settling' had conspired to give the roof of my cottage a peculiar twisted appearance – a decidedly odd look which was unique simply because it was unlikely that anyone would wish to replicate the design. Indeed I was once referred to as 'the crooked man in the crooked house' by one of the editors of 'Whittingfun'. However, architectural monstrosity or not, the house became a popular landmark on the treasure hunting trail and hence during a warm summer or autumn Sunday afternoon I might receive some twenty or so groups of treasure hunters all of whom would ask the reason for the crooked roof and advice concerning the next 'clue' on the road to Whittington – which was normally Mrs Harrison's delightful cottage a half mile distant.

I am usually remarkably patient with these treasure hunters, indeed an extremely vulnerable eccentric's best defence is his patience and tolerance, but on that particular Sunday, my nerves stretched taut by two sleepless nights and my body still tingling with the results of my encounter with the nettle patch, I confess I was somewhat less than tolerant with the procession of visitors that plagued me on that bright Sunday afternoon.

As each and every treasure hunting car party pulled up outside the cottage and the giggling navigator surveyed my twisted roof and knocked on the door to enquire about a clue, Khan, the larger of the Dobermanns launched himself at the ornamental door, screaming execrations at the intruders and producing vibrations in the house which would have registered on the Richter scale. Not one of the navigators persisted after Khan struck the door, roaring in fury, but it would be only minutes before the next carload of treasure hunters arrived and the din began again. I penned the set of short stories entitled *Adventures of an Artisan Hunter* that weekend. It is a curious book with a somewhat jerky prose style, perhaps readers can now understand why! However, my nightmare was only just beginning, for I had yet to leave the dogs to their own devices for any length of time.

Monday morning found me exhausted and sleep-shotten, for the dogs paced ceaselessly in the corridor all night, resting not an instance, or so it seemed. I dressed, shaved without looking in the mirror, for I felt I would have aged considerably since the arrival of the Dobermanns and I didn't need my reflection to confirm my theories concerning the ageing process. I walked the pair to the end of my lane, drinking my tea as I did so and prepared for another one of 'those days' at school.

Looking back on my days teaching in Walsall I am amazed at how I survived the time and remained even moderately sane. Later, just prior to the closure of Forest Comprehensive, the newspapers were unkind enough to label the place as 'the worst school in the Midlands'. Teaching in such a place was hard, tiring and at times soul destroying. I kept order simply because I knew the district, liked the people and had a street knowledge few teachers had or considered worth acquiring. My classes were always the most disruptive and in order to maintain an acceptable level of attendance it was necessary to fetch members of my class from their homes each morning. Left to their own devices my classes refused to attend school and spent the day engaging in an orgy of shoplifting and car theft. If I was away for any length of time my class attendance figures fell to less than twenty-five percent, although, frankly, many of the staff were glad when some of the most disruptive children stayed away. If certain boys were absent, the crime figures for the district rose sharply. If certain girls failed to turn up, they would be soliciting. We had no real drugs problem in the school (although glue sniffing enjoyed a short-lived, somewhat blissful, period of popularity) simply because a desperate, depressing poverty seemed to hold the district in its thrall.

Staff earned every penny of their salaries in such a school despite the establishment's appalling examination results and it was not unknown for a young, enthusiastic teacher embarking on his probationary year to leave during the lunchtime of his first day, overwhelmed by the tumult and chaos which characterised the place. Those teachers who stayed adopted the posture of a journeyman prize fighter, simply riding the punches life threw and hanging on until offered early retirement or in many cases medical discharge and death. Students on teaching practice dreaded coming to the school. School inspectors simply regarded the place as an embarrassment and left without criticising too much, for few of these inspectors could have survived a day teaching at the establishment. Thus each day seemed like an eternity and I always arrived home desperately tired with sharp pains in my chest and down my left arm – warning signs perhaps, but at the time at least, signs I chose to ignore.

I often pulled up outside my cottage and fell asleep at the wheel – sometimes with the engine still running only to awaken, stiff and sore, to go to clean and feed my dogs. On the day in question, I arrived home to find my end of day reverie interrupted by the cacophonous baying of the two Dobermanns who were engaging in throwing themselves at the ornamental front door – or to be more precise what was left of my ornamental front door.

I opened the door and groaned as I beheld the spectacle of my living room. There is some doubt as to which breeds were used to create the Dobermann but I suspect beaver blood played a great part in the development of the breed. I glanced in horror at the damage wrought to my lovely front door – a door for which I had saved long and hard to buy. Great slashes had been ripped out of it and the pair had obviously taken some pains to mutilate the doorpost as well. My wooden rocking chair, a present from some Godchildren I had taught and who considered I was sufficiently geriatric to merit such a present, was wrecked, chewed almost to matchwood by the pair of lunatic dogs.

What was even worse was the awful stench which permeated the house. Despite the fact that my guards had been allowed out to perform their bodily functions earlier that day, they had fouled in several places and their infernal pacing had distributed the mess fairly evenly around my corridor and living room. I am accustomed to foul smells – indeed I once hunted rats on a maggot factory – yet the vile stench within my home made me gag and I had to clean and disinfect the mess even before I switched on my kettle to make tea.

Amidst the hybrid stench of Jeyes Fluid and dog excrement – a truly objectionable olfactory chimera – I sat down to take stock of the carnage the pair had caused and contemplated as to whether the burglars were preferable to Dobermanns. Determined that as I had bought the pair, so now I must tolerate their idiosyncrasies or accept the fact that my home was open house to every burglar who fancied a spot of housebreaking. I drank my tea, which tasted of carbolic acid and ate my food, which savoured of something even less pleasant, and decided to spend the evening in another room where the vile odours could not permeate.

I tolerated stench and destruction for a full month before I finally gave in and kennelled the Dobermanns outside. Each day I would return home to find quite serious damage to my place and property, moan a little, sit with my head between my hands awhile, cursing police inefficiency and then set to cleaning up the filth and attempting to mask the fearsome stench with an even more malodourous disinfectant. Mo Smith, a settled Romany, my constant companion during those awful days, refrained from coming in the house, complaining the place stank like a knacker's yard for elderly donkeys, and, while I could not disagree with him, I felt his comments were hurtful, to say the least. Yet the stench was appalling and on one day in that fine autumn I could savour the foul odour emanating from the house even before I reached the porch – 'You could use a skunk as an air freshener in this 'ouse,' Mo said.

Frankly, matters came to a head when I returned home to find that my burglars, thwarted by my Dobermanns perhaps, had in a fit of pique hurled stones through the windows of my home, littering the rooms with broken glass through which the Dobermanns had trampled, leaving bloody pad marks throughout my house. Eddie succinct and logical as ever had suggested that now my burglars had decided it was a shade dangerous to raid my home it was time to transfer one or both of the brutes to the run and get a German Shepherd Dog bitch puppy, run her on, get her to develop a guarding instinct and then by dint of allowing the German Shepherd Dog to run free, use the bitch to protect the premises and the rest of the dogs.

In despair I replaced the glass, built new shutters on the outside of the house windows and, without further ado, set about searching for a suitable German Shepherd Dog bitch puppy. I should like to be able to say that I deliberated on my choice of puppy carefully, selecting my breeder, checking his or her credentials and finally, after much consideration, choosing my puppy. However, this would be a lie. After seeing an advertisement in *Exchange And Mart* I phoned a breeder near Manchester, travelled the hundred or so miles north, saw the litter and selected a white bitch from a mixed litter of white and coloured puppies. It was one of those impromptu chance purchases that have punctuated my erratic lifestyle, but, on reflection, possibly the best buy I have ever made, and here I suppose begins my story proper.

CHAPTER 4

Colour Prejudice

Eddie eyed my white puppy critically, examining it with care, before uttering a word, 'The best protection dog I have ever seen was a white bitch,' he stated with some deliberation, but added 'but you'll find some opposition to white or cream puppies in the German Shepherd Dog fraternity. Come to think of it,' he continued, 'there is considerable colour prejudice within the dog world.'

Eddie as usual was correct. At one time white or cream coloured German Shepherd Dogs abounded in Germany and were commonly used by shepherds to herd and drive (there is a difference) sheep and cattle. In fact, one of the ancestors of the modern German Shepherd Dog was a white male called rather unoriginally Pilot and, hence, white German Shepherd Dog puppies appeared in most of the early litters of puppies. However, a standard of excellence was drawn up the German breeders with customary Prussian precision, excluding the white animals by stating that white animals were not desirable. Whereupon, the breeders became intensely hostile to white puppies, destroying them at birth, and often denying that the sires and dams of litters carried white or cream genes. A white-producing stud dog was avoided (although one of the great German Shepherd Dogs, Bandit Von Leiberg carried these white genes) and eschewing the use of bitches which had produced white or cream puppies. In fact such is the superstitious, unscientific claptrap which pervades dog breeding (and nowhere is ignorance as bliss as in dogdom) that while a German Shepherd Dog breeder might accept taunts that his mother was a slattern, his father a wastrel and his wife a tart, he would seek legal redress should someone suggest his stud dog carried white genes.

Yet there is not the slightest evidence to suggest that white German Shepherd Dogs are a whit inferior to their coloured littermates, either physically or mentally. White German Shepherd Dogs grow at the same rate as do their coloured siblings and are equally as acute and lusty. They are no more prone to hip dysplasia or epilepsy, two ailments to which German Shepherd Dogs as a breed, at one time at least, seemed all too prone, than coloured puppies of the same breeding.

Yet it is a fact that shepherds in Western Europe seem a shade antipathetic to white herding dogs or dogs which have a large proportion of white in their colour patterns. It is often quite difficult to home collies which are white-faced, for apparently few sheep are intimidated by the stare of a white-faced collie. Yet such collies, particularly white-faced beardies of certain strains, are tigers when herding and refrain from backing down to even belligerent and forceful black face rams.

It has, however, been argued that white herding dogs are commonly used in Southern and Eastern Europe where Maremmas, Kuvasz and Pyrenean mountain dogs can still be seen herding, though scarcely distinguishable from the sheep they are tending. However, the role of these sheepdogs is vastly different from that of the Border collie or the German Shepherd Dog and so for that matter is the training and rearing afforded these huge white sheepdogs.

Wolves became extinct in England in the 16th century, although perhaps solitary specimens lived out a lonely, miserable existence in some remote mountainous fastness until they too died of old age or fell victim to some trophy hunter who was anxious to enter posterity as being the hunter who slew the last wolf in the county. Hence English sheepdogs were seldom required to guard flocks from large predators but are used mainly to herd and drive sheep and cattle. Smaller sheepdogs, dogs which required smaller rations but yet were large enough to inspire fear in the sheep, were therefore developed by shepherds and drovers, although many of the bearded collies of Scotland are still extremely courageous and willing to face down intruders. Indeed some of the larger strains of bearded collie are ferocious guard dogs and are instantly able to detect the presence of any person who may be hostile to the dogs' owners.

However, in Southern and Eastern Europe wolves still abounded until the turn of the present century and became very numerous in the wake of the two world wars which swept the continent. Hence the role of the sheepdogs used in these areas was different. These sheepdogs were required to guard the flocks as much as herd and to drive them and hence white animals which could mingle with the sheep without disturbing them were favoured by shepherds. In fact most shepherds went to considerable effort to ensure the dogs were well and truly integrated into the flocks. Puppies were separated from their dams at a few weeks of age, gelded and put to be suckled by ewes. The puppies were not allowed to mingle with or associate with other dogs and became very attached to the sheep they were guarding, so attached in fact that they would attack any wolf, dog or human intruder who threatened the flock. This peculiar imprinting had been practised for hundreds of years in wolf-infested Europe and Darwin mentions the practice in his description of the Patagonian shepherds and their dogs, for this method of rearing sheepdogs had been imported from Spain together with bearded collie-type herding dogs.

However, the British have always been decidedly suspicious of white dogs and have always regarded white sports appearing in litters of coloured puppies as being of inferior quality. At one time it was popularly believed that a white bull terrier was invariably a deaf bull terrier, for a certain splendid and prepotent bull terrier bred some totally deaf progeny. In fact in the 1930s bull terrier breeders often advised the occasional dash of brindled bull terrier blood to maintain the breed's constitutional vigour.

The suspicion bull terrier fanciers displayed towards white dogs may well have had its origins in some concrete fact however. The English bull terrier had been bred, at least in part, by mating bulldog type dogs with that curious and effete enigma, the white English terrier, a breed which had a fearsome reputation for producing hereditary faults and infertility (this caused the eclipse of the breed in the early 1900s). Some of these creatures were true 'fanciers' dogs', nesh, suffering badly from the cold and most wore woollen jackets as a protection against winter chills.

In Scotland, a far cry from the London public houses where the tiny white English terrier was commonly seen, shepherds and sportsmen alike were deeply suspicious of white terriers born to coloured parents. When Scottish terriers produced white offspring it was customary to dispose of these white whelps at birth for they were believed to be constitutionally inferior to their coloured nest-mates. This has changed and it is said that Malcolm of Poltalloch kept only white terriers after a favourite fawn-coloured dog had been mistaken for a fox and shot, but at that time several breeders were producing and keeping white Scottish terriers. Captain Keene bred and exhibited white 'Scotties' and later Dr Flaxman bred Pittenweem terriers from a dark Scottish bitch which always produced a white puppy or so in her litters. Flaxman's terriers, which were known as Pittenweem terriers, did not enjoy great popularity, but the white sports bred by Colonel Ian Malcolm were to become the foundation stock for the West Highland White terrier.

On the subject of their being a grain of truth in most 'doggy' legends, it is perhaps reasonable to conclude this brief chapter with a reference to the belief that white working collies are invariably blind or deaf, or sometimes blind and deaf. Now the curious merle colouration found in certain strains of collie is a bit of a puzzle. When merle collies are mated to non-merle coloured mates a normal litter is born from the union, some of the puppies of which are merle in colour. However, when a merle collie is mated to another merle, certain puppies will be white and these whelps will be blind, deaf or blind and deaf. It is often quite difficult to tell if certain collies are merle, for as a puppy grows the merle colouration will often be masked. Yet the animal is genetically a merle, indeed even the liver of a merle coloured puppy is dappled, and when such an apparently non-merle animal is mated to another merle curiously deformed puppies are produced.

A similar factor is found in white blue-eyed Persian cats, which are invariably deaf. When odd-eyed Persian specimens are born the ear nearest the blue eye is usually deaf. Hence there is a grain of truth, but no more than a grain I'm afraid, that all white coloured animals are defective or constitutionally unsound in some way or other.

However, few German Shepherd Dogs are white and the majority of 'white' German Shepherd Dogs are really pale cream in colour. Yet there is still an antipathy to pale coloured German Shepherd Dogs amongst the German Shepherd Dog breeders fraternity – although curiously in the 1990s, a Seiger show (Seiger means literally 'the very best of the very best') for white German Shepherd Dogs was held in Germany. Not surprisingly the exhibits had been imported to Germany from Britain and America where it is not 'verboten' to breed such colours. America does, in fact, produce some very fine strains of white German Shepherd Dogs. Yet German German Shepherd Dog breeders still continue to destroy white puppies in the nest and to deny that their dogs carry these 'white genes', so a dichotomy between the white German Shepherd Dog and its darker coloured form continues to widen, at least on the continent of Europe.

However, by now the reader must be confused by the strange and exotic sounding jargon concerning the breed, so at this point perhaps it is expedient to discuss the German Shepherd Dog before proceeding further with my tale – and in doing so I hope to unravel and explain the hopeless tangle of jargon which apparently is part and parcel of the world of German Shepherd Dog breeding, showing and working.

CHAPTER 5

The German Shepherd Dog

To begin at the beginning in true Dylan Thomas fashion, the ancestor of all domesticated dogs is said to be some form of wolf, although three species of wolf supposedly gave rise to the various diverse breeds of dog. The northern wolf, Canis lupus lupus, supposedly gave rise to the various breeds of northern shepherding dogs, such as collies and the German Shepherd Dog and others, while the hounds and mastiffs are reputedly descended from the huge broad-skulled Tibetan wolves, creatures which harried the travellers on the caravan route popularly known as the Silk Road. The sighthounds, long, slender, speedy dogs such as the greyhound, the saluki and the borzoi are reputedly descended from the slinky, pale footed Asiatic wolf, Canis lupus pallipis. Such are the classifications of dogs according to Richard and Alice Fiennes in their noteworthy and much quoted book *The Natural History Of The Dog* (1968), but it is just possible that the Fiennes were wrong and another wild species of canid gave rise to the domesticated dog.

It is quite likely that a wild species of dog similar in size, type, shape and disposition to the feral Australian dog, the dingo, was the forebear of the various breeds of dog and that prior to domestication proper and the totally predictable domestication pattern suggested by Zeuner, the ancestors of dogs enjoyed the wild/domesticate/feral/wild life cycle of the dingo before the colonisation of the Antipodes by Europeans.

Strebel is of the opinion that the ancestors of the German Shepherd

Dog were spitz-tailed (having a curly tail similar to the tail carried by native Arctic sled dogs) and such a tail is sported by the dingo and related species of feral or semi-wild canids. Strebel is of the opinion that while the early breeders of German Shepherd Dogs were tolerant of such tails, providing that is, that the dog was capable of performing its duties as a guard and herding dog. Once breeders began to see the dog as an object of beauty as well as usefulness the curled spitz tail became aesthetically unappealing and men hence set to breed out this curled tail and so the German Shepherd Dog took on a slightly more lupine appearance.

Yet despite the appellation 'the Alsatian wolf dog', once afforded the breed by some war writers, the German Shepherd Dog bears little resemblance to the northern wolf, although it is likely that breeders have deliberately, or perhaps unintentionally, produced a dog which bears a slight resemblance to the wolf. The early specimens of the breed had a far less lupine appearance than modern German Shepherd Dogs. Strebel tells a fascinating and fanciful tale of one of the early Alsatians, Phylax Von Eulau, who was shown at Dresden early in the 20th century. The dog excited great fury from the benched borzois bred at the famous Perchino kennels in Russia. Strebel suggests that the fury of the hounds was due to the fact that they 'smelled the wolf blood' in the Alsatian/German Shepherd Dog but Strebel clearly knew nothing of the peculiarities of sighthounds. Greyhounds, salukis, borzois and even the more placid whippets will often display a furious antipathy to certain individual dogs which manifest some peculiarity or adopt some unusual stance or habit and will erupt furiously and volubly when they see the particular dog, although they will often be indifferent to a dog which, to the casual eye, is identical to the animal which has triggered the antipathy. One often hears tales related by greyhound trainers of dogs which display furious aggression towards certain breeds of dog yet ignore dogs of like size and colour.

Early German Shepherd Dogs were a somewhat mixed bunch and very mixed in type, colour and size. Indeed Fred L. Lanting in his book *The Total German Shepherd Dog* shows photographs of merle coloured German Shepherd Dogs and rough-coated animals of the same breed, which bore some resemblance to prick-eared Airedales. However, once Von Stephanitz decided on a standard of excellence for the breed, the modern type of dog began to evolve, both quickly and systematically, particularly once Von Stephanitz acquired the dog Horand and used the beast at stud to fix a type. Horand was considered quite a big dog at the time, scaling in at 24" at the shoulder, but he was a fearless, happy dog with a pleasant, sociable disposition. Within a dozen years or so the breed had evolved to produce a type of dog which could instantly be identified as a German Shepherd Dog, but it required the Great War to show the incredible versatility of the breed,

The First World War has often been described as the struggle between the Airedale and the German Shepherd Dog by doggy writers. At the onset of hostilities, and possibly long before Princeps fired his first starting shot, Britain and Germany had started to train war dogs, which were seldom required to be hostile on the battlefield but were required to run messages between the lines, braving a hail of machine gun bullets, to transport panniers full of ammunition and medical supplies and to detect trapped soldiers and civilians buried under mounds of debris and mud.

Britain enlisted the services of the largest of terriers, namely the Airedale, supposedly the result of mating an otterhound with a bull terrier, and one of the greatest exponents at utilising the ability of the Airedale was Lt. Colonel Richardson who in 1924 published a decidedly avant-garde and sophisticated book *Watch Dogs – Their Training And Management*. Richardson had considerable experience at training this alert and game dog and taught the dogs a variety of skills ranging from guard work to search and rescue techniques. Richardson did in fact perfect a technique of teaching dogs to seek out certain explosive substances but more on this subject later.

Germany enlisted the services of over 28,000 war dogs, most of which were German Shepherd Dogs, and if the breed's abilities were known to the British prior to 1914 by the cessation of the war there were few British servicemen who were not aware of the incredible intelligence possessed by these dogs. While there is little doubt that the Airedale of 1914 was a far more valiant creature than the German Shepherd Dog, and was gamer and harder biting, few wartime veterans returned home with anything but praise for the intelligence and versatility of the German dog.

On the subject of the German dog it is perhaps expedient to mention the incredible hostility the British manifested to anything German during the conflict. Shortly after the shelling of Scarborough the British press released such a hail of anti-German propaganda (most of which had little substance in fact, one must add) that anyone with Teutonic connections quaked with fear. Yards of tiny inoffensive dachshunds were clubbed to death or poisoned, blissfully unaware of their Germanic origins and it became expedient for owners of German Shepherd Dogs to refer to their dogs, rather inaccurately, as Alsatians, though the breed had little connection with that much disputed territory of Alsace

Lorraine. Hence until the 1960s the German Shepherd Dog was referred to as the Alsatian, or more inaccurately still, the Alsatian wolf dog until Britain once again returned to its senses, shed its ridiculous xenophobia, and used the correct title for this very noble looking dog.

Sir Jocelyn Lucas MC told a curious tale which clearly indicates the incredible intelligence of the breed. Lucas had been captured by the Germans early in the war and, as he had developed gangrene in his toes, he was considered as little threat by his captors who allowed Lucas greater liberty than they allowed his more able-bodied comrades. During Lucas' imprisonment he witnessed several POWs secreting German uniforms in readiness for an escape back to British lines and several POWs even took to mingling with German soldiers to test the efficacy of their disguises. Lucas said that such stunts were quite possible after a particularly savage bombardment left the German lines stunned, bewildered and disorganised. However, on the day in question the soldiers and their impersonators were called to order in a long line, and a dog handler, German Shepherd Dog on leash, examined the assembled troops. The dog stopped at every imposter and barked loudly but ignored genuine German troops. Lucas suggested that as the POWs were fed a slightly different diet from regular troops the dog was alerted by the distinctive body odour emitted by the POWs, who were led away and punished as soon as they were detected.

I hate leaving a tale unfinished, particularly a tale of this nature. Lucas amputated his own gangrenous toes, some say with a scalpel made from the lid of a sardine tin and escaped to join up with the British Forces. He was an incredible man by any standards.

On the subject of the terrible bombardment which preceded every attack, whole villages were often flattened by the barrage and people often became trapped in the ruins of houses etc.. Both Airedales and German Shepherd Dogs were trained to find people trapped under the debris that resulted from the bombardment and the method used to train these rescue dogs was identical to that used by the monks who dwelled in the Augustinian monastery of St. Bernard, a hospice standing 8,200 feet above sea level and here once again I crave the reader's indulgence while I describe the methods used by these monks, who trained huge red and white mastiffs to seek out travellers buried in the snows near the St. Bernard Pass.

A monk would rear and train such a mastiff and once the dog had formed a good relationship with the monk, rescue training would commence. A hole would be dug in snow and while the dog was restrained by another handler, the trainer would run and hide in the hole. The mastiff was then released and would run and find the trainer who would enthuse and praise the animal for its efforts. This game would be repeated every day until the mastiff became excited by the prospect of the exercise.

The trainer would now cover himself with a light layer of snow and once more the dog would be sent to find him and be encouraged to unearth the buried trainer, who would praise and pet the animal for its efforts. However, now the trainer would enlist the services of yet another enthusiast, who would join the trainer in the hole, lying atop of the handler under a light layer of snow. The dog would once again be sent to find the handler and would be rather surprised to find the monk secreted beneath another man – still monastic life is always a little strange one supposes! The game would be repeated often and the assistant changed from time to time to confuse the dog.

The trainer now comes out of the hole and the mastiff would be sent to seek out strangers buried under snow, receiving praise, petting and food for its efforts. Thereafter, if travellers were reported lost, the dog, (minus its traditional bottle of brandy, which was never used to fortify victims incidentally) would seek out and dig to find the hidden bodies of travellers. It is interesting to note again that as mentioned earlier, despite its obvious mastiff shape and great size the dog doesn't possess the awesome visage sported by most mastiffs and has a 'kind and gentle face'.

Both German and British war dog trainers adapted the methods of these Alpine monks to train dogs to search for those trapped beneath rubble or mud. Illtyd Thomas, an eloquent Welsh miner, recalls the day when he became buried beneath earth and mud during the first days of the German counteroffensive in 1916. 'I had been hurled into a ditch by a shell blast and covered by earth, mud and broken duckboard. Mud was beginning to fill the spaces around my body and I felt a curious weariness which prepared me for death. A dog, possibly a large terrier or crossbred collie, began to dig to me and to bark happily as it unearthed my muddy face. I could not believe my good luck and chatted to the rescue team as it proceeded to dig me out. It was several minutes before I realised I had lost both my legs!'

If I might leap ahead two or so decades, the Golden Age (if such times could ever be referred to as golden years) of the rescue dog was surely the time of the Blitz during World War II. Some of the best rescue/detection dogs were trained during these days – and Heaven knows such dogs had ample opportunity to practice their skills in the war-torn cities of Britain and Germany. In these circumstances the

German Shepherd Dogs had ample chance to demonstrate their seeking abilities themselves. Great trainers, such as Mrs Griffin, whose dogs were registered under the Crumstone prefix, worked tirelessly with these rescue dogs seeking the bodies of those trapped beneath the bomb-damaged rubble. One of Mrs Griffin's dogs Crumstone Danko was reputed to be able to scale up to 16 feet 4 inches in addition to being a competent rescue dog.

However it was, as could be expected, in Germany that the incredible working ability of the German Shepherd Dog was best exploited and just as Teutonic science students deliberately acquire all the scientific qualifications that will fit on a sheet of paper, so many German Shepherd Dog trainers seek to acquire sundry qualifications for their dogs. German breeders virtually expect their German Shepherd Dogs to be able to protect their owners and families, so they stage Schutzhund (or protection dog) stakes so that dogs can qualify as protection guards. These schutzhund tests involve obedience work, tracking ability and above all protection work, so the Schutzhund III test requires a dog which performs several obedience, tracking work and protection displays of the highest order. What is most extraordinary is the fact that most Seigers and Seigerins are also trained to SCH III standards and are capable of working well, in addition to being aesthetically pleasing.

However, German breeders and handlers are often reluctant to merely train their German Shepherd Dogs to the high standards required by the SCH III tests and often take the training of their dogs a stage or several stages further. It is not uncommon to find outstanding German dogs having not only SCH III qualifications but also other indications of the dog's working ability indicated by a variety of letters as part of its pedigree.

The letters AD indicate the dog or bitch has passed a physical endurance test, gaiting for nine miles, followed by an obedience test, after which the dog must pass a physical examination by a qualified person.

BLH or BFH indicate that the dog has qualified as a guide dog to assist blind people – this is a seldom seen qualification, as it requires very specific training. DH indicates the dog has been trained as a service dog and this qualification is not uncommonly seen on certain pedigrees.

FH indicates that the dog has passed a tracking dog examination while GvH means the dog has been trained for border patrol work. HGH shows that the dog has been trained as a herding dog, but here the person examining the pedigree should proceed with caution. While it seems impossible not to eulogise about German training methods or on the incredible versatility of the German Shepherd Dog, to compare the herding instinct of these dogs with those of the native British breeds of collie, the Border and the now rather rare working bearded collie, is ludicrous, for while German Shepherd Dogs can be taught to herd quite effectively and to drive cattle fairly well, the German Shepherd Dog lacks the finely honed herding ability of a good working Border or bearded collie.

PH indicates the dog has been trained to the standard required as a police dog, while PDH indicates the animal has not only been trained to the required standard but is serving as a police dog. A further police dog qualification is PFP I or PFP II which indicates the animal has expertise as a tracking dog or police tracker dog, while PSP I or PSP II is awarded to those dogs which have great expertise in police orientated manwork.

Less common is the SH qualification which indicates the dog has been used by the Red Cross or similar organisations as an ambulance dog, particularly during wartime years.

A more common qualification is Such H, a qualification which is won by tracking dogs and is earned by taking part in sports qualifications. ZH I and ZH II is a qualification carried by customs dogs, dogs which are expert in seeking out the presence of narcotics or explosives in luggage and elsewhere. Here perhaps the reader will forgive a slight digression while I explain how these truly remarkable dogs are usually trained to perform their extraordinary work. These dogs never display the slightest antipathy towards those who are actively engaged in smuggling drugs or explosives. On the contrary, such dogs are usually delighted to see people carrying these substances – and here lies the secret in training such animals. Dogs which are required to seek out such substances are usually given a particular toy and encouraged to become almost fixated by such a toy. The 'toy' is now impregnated with the scent of the particular drug or explosive and the toy returned to the dog who is ecstatic at having his beloved plaything given back to it. Hence when the dog is taken to a position where the particular drug or explosive is thought to be present the dog becomes wild with delight and seeks out the substance, as the animal believes that this particular drug or explosive indicates the presence of its beloved toy. Hence it is not unusual to find a drug seeking dog greeting a drug or explosives carrying miscreant like and old and much loved friend, for he believes the smuggler is in possession of its toy.

A dog seeks out a particular substance, or rather seeks out the presence or a particular substance with which its toy has been impregnated. Thus, a dog which has been trained to seek out the presence of a toy impregnated with Semtex may well overlook a canister of black powder, chemically different but still explosive. A dog trained to seek out the rather pungent narcotic marijuana may also pass a huge haul of heroin or cocaine. There is a tale, albeit a tale I believe to be apocryphal, of a dog trained to seek out cannabis, or marijuana, which became ecstatic when a warehouse containing burning sacks was approached. Hemp sacks are made of fibres of another species of cannabis, which has a slightly similar scent to cannabis indicus, or marijuana.

I now conclude this list of qualifications with mention of Zpr which, strictly speaking, is not a qualification but an indication that the animal has passed a breed survey and is thus suitable for breeding and continuing its bloodlines.

This now concludes this chapter concerning the general qualities of the German Shepherd Dog and I shall return, post haste, to the subject of my white German Shepherd Dog bitch, Polly.

CHAPTER 6

Polly Arrives

I now resume the tale of the white German Shepherd Dog puppy I purchased. The colour was given something of a boost by a rather silly film called *White Dog*, a tale of a white German Shepherd Dog which was encouraged by a family of redneck white racists to attack black people, but to be totally steady in the presence of even the smallest white baby. I hadn't seen the film but I was made aware of the plot by a somewhat bizarre and humorous incident in my classroom.

The school in which I was teaching at the time I bought Polly was outrageous by any standards. Discipline, if it ever had existed, had long since been forgotten and it was expedient to simply enter my classroom, close the doors and keep out of the sheer bedlam which raged in the rest of the school. Staff standards had slipped and I found that the majority of the staff had also chosen the splendid isolationism I had sought to adopt. Conflicts between disruptives and those of the staff who still tried to maintain discipline were all too common and the end of the day bell found the staff running like track greyhounds for their cars and racing through the school gates. Morale was low and I confess I kept discipline in my class simply because I knew the children's parents and often went to tea at various houses in the district. However, like the rest of the staff, I child-minded and survived, teaching little perhaps but not experiencing the terrible mental strain that afflicted many of the staff.

The day in question was little different from any other day. The same battle for survival was played out by those staff who still demanded some element of discipline to be extant in their classrooms while sheer chaos prevailed in the corridors as recalcitrant teenagers declined to go to lessons. My own class had settled down to a moderate state of frenzy but before I could attempt to teach them – magnificent hyperbole – a blond, Aryan-type boy burst into the classroom, barred the door and began shouting, 'Black bastards' at a crowd of coloured children, one of whom was my Godchild, who then attempted to break down the door and attack the name-calling racist. Tipper, as the boy was called, began yelling a series of epithets that would have drawn a blush from a New York longshoreman. I didn't attempt to stop the youth – I had long since discovered the futility of stopping such a madman in mid-flight – and merely waited until he had exhausted himself trying to barricade the door. Indeed people who believe that programmes like 'Grange Hill' are too violent to be realistic would do well to visit an establishment of the type I have described.

Tipper finished piling the desks across the doorway, and exhausted by his efforts fell across the furniture, almost too breathless to speak. He turned to assess into which class he had forced an entry and seemed almost pleased to see me. He sauntered breathlessly to my desk and began his schpiel, hardly pausing to draw breath as he did so. 'Yer know that video White Dog, sir,' (he didn't wait for me to affirm I had seen the film), 'S'bout a white dog, a German Shepherd Alsatian, sir, that kills blacks, tears them to pieces,' he continued, 'but it don't touch white people.' He gave an impersonation of a huge dog dismantling, filleting and jointing a terrified Negro – he paused a second and with his head held on one side he uttered, 'You breed those, sir – d'yer sell 'em?' – hopeful perhaps of acquiring such a beast and being able to amble home over mounds of mangled black enemies.

Tipper had not yet met Polly (although he had heard I had such a dog) and if he had he would have been horrified at her thoroughly 'wimpish' attitude to life. German Shepherd Dogs mature slowly and are very infantile and timid during their growing up period. If stepped on quite accidentally she screamed as though thrashed and continued to bleat piteously long after any other breed of dog had forgotten the incident. The slightest sign of possible injury produced a plaintive screaming sound and once in Lichfield Shopping Precinct, when a young child stepped on her toes, she bleated and screamed so loudly that an irate woman, who had not witnessed the incident, raced across and threatened to attack me for ill-treating the dog. Come to think of it, I wonder how many RSPCA complaints have been brought simply because people didn't witness a particular incident or hadn't the common-sense to realise what had caused some animal to emit a cry of pain.

I was not the only creature to cause Polly to scream with pain and fear. One day a pitiful shriek caused me to race out to my garden to investigate the cause of the scream. I found Polly howling in pain and a large wounded crow, wing held at a curious angle, hiding near the fence. I guessed that Polly had seen the creature, tried to make friends with it and been rewarded with a stinging peck to the face. Her face showed only a slight abrasion but she continued to squeal with pain for hours after the attack. A terrier puppy of the same age, overmatched by a large rat, would have forgotten the encounter in minutes despite the painful bite rats inflict, but then terriers are made of sterner stuff than Polly. She was, at this stage of her life at least, a far cry from the destroyer of anything with even a hint of coloured blood featured in the video *White Dog*, although I confess I have only recently seen the film.

Yet I have never owned a puppy that was more perspicacious and receptive to training than Polly. I have always believed that Polly's almost supernatural ability to learn was simply due to her great desire to please. If I taught her a simple task and displayed any pleasure at her success at performing that task, she would attempt to perform that task again and again if only to see my display of approval. 'Sit', down training was accomplished in a single wet afternoon although staying put while I walked away from her distressed her greatly, for she had an almost slavish desire to be with me. Funnily enough, most Shepherds, coloured and white, are unhappy at staying at the down position while their owners walk out of sight.

She took to retrieving like a bird dog as soon as she realised that the action of carrying an object pleased me, and as soon as I returned home from school she simply ran to fetch some object, carrying the article in her mouth until I engaged her in a game. She proved an absolute delight to own and a pleasure to train and Polly's presence made life bearable as conditions at the school worsened.

In hominid social groups it is customary to find scapegoats to blame as soon as a social situation becomes unbearable. An outburst of typhoid in a Bantu village was usually treated not by herbal medicine but by lining up the villagers while a juju man walks along the line sniffing out who was responsible for introducing the malaise. The poor wretch, once identified, was pounded to death or meted out some other ghastly fate, while the rest of the tribe were either forced to attend the spectacle or, as was often the case, gleefully joined in the poor wretch's destruction. The chances are that while the death of the victim was unlikely to cause the epidemic to abate, the ghastly spectacle allowed the onlookers to feel some jubilation at the death of one of their neighbours.

As civilisation advanced a little, the scent hunting juju man's services were dispensed with and victims with certain physical or social peculiarities were offered up as votive sacrifices to appease some invisible force which brought disaster or catastrophe. Old women with bad disfigurement were usually the first to suffer when a purge began but it was not long before the community began to mark out members of the group who were different or displayed different interests which set them apart from the group. During the Inquisitions when Christendom displayed an almost hysterical hatred against anyone who today would be described simply as an oddball, people with warts or birthmarks between their nipples were eagerly sought by the Inquisition and made to suffer unbelievable tortures.

Matters are sometimes much the same in the teaching profession, particularly if members of that profession have seen little of life and have scampered from school through college and back to school. Indeed, there is a great deal of truth in the statement 'A man amongst children becomes a child amongst men'. Teachers who have experienced this lifestyle and only this lifestyle, often become childish, peevish and also malicious, setting about less fortunate colleagues with an unwholesome frenzy until the said colleague becomes a pathetic, snivelling remnant of what a man should be and slinks and slithers out of the profession to seek other employment.

I became aware of the arrival of the Inquisition when I found a forty-year-old colleague snivelling piteously in the staff toilets, lamenting the fact he had been pressured by the powers that be to leave the profession.

I was always rather careful about my future when I saw such a purge being conducted as I was acutely aware that, because of my own idiosyncrasies, it was only a matter of time before the same Inquisitors start paying attention to me. Hence I began to enlarge my social life and no longer stayed on in the school for extracurricular duties – not that extracurricular activities still existed, for the purge had set member of staff against member of staff and school dances, discos and other social events were terminated abruptly. One of the more forgiving and gentle members of the staff attempted to run one discotheque only to be so savagely assaulted by a gang of the children that he spent time in hospital – and after this calamity the staff ceased to run any out of school activity and vied with each other to be first out of the school gates when the bell rang.

I became one of the leading contenders to be into fourth gear before the school bell stopped reverberating and I raced home to my beloved dogs. I have often felt that the breakdown of the social life of the school contributed the fact that I trained Polly to a very high standard and developed an unusual relationship with her. I have kept dogs long enough to avoid being even slightly anthropomorphic about the subject of dog training but at times it did appear that she knew exactly what I was thinking and sympathised with my problems. In fact, now that I am able to reflect on those horrid years towards the end of my teaching career, I'm sure Polly kept me fairly sane when I too attracted the attention of the Inquisition. That, however, is another tale and one I have related in another book if I remember correctly.

Polly plodded along patiently behind me following me from one room to another, never leaving me for a moment, and while I became only too aware that she was a far cry from being the guard dog I required she was the most desirable companion imaginable. She asked for little other than food, friendship and a warm place to sleep and in exchange gave the most unbelievable loyalty and quiet companionship, but it took me some time to realise the untapped lode of abilities she had.

At that time I lived on a quiet country lane in Lichfield, a half mile or so from the Whittington canal and one of the skills I allowed a puppy to learn was that it could not walk on water – I'll explain.

Every puppy I ever owned, until that time, would, on first seeing the

canal – which was algae-covered in summer – attempt to race across the surface only to sink like a stone, and emerge with a look of shock and bewilderment on its face. However Polly was different. As we approached the canal bank she became aware of my interest in the algae-covered surface and sniffed the waters as if to assess the nature of the substance below the algae. I believe I laughed, and then flung a flat stone that splashed ducks and drakes fashion across the green waters of the canal and landed on the other side.

To my utter amazement Polly touched the water with her paw as if to assess its physical properties and then quietly slid into the waters as fluidly as would a seal. Awe-struck, I stood watching as Polly clambered from the waters on the other side, shook herself, slowly sought out the stone I had thrown and returned with it across the canal. I could not have been more surprised, Polly was four months old at the time and totally unaware of how dangerous deep water could be. Yet she performed her retrieve as well as would a Labrador puppy of twice her age and gently dropped the flat pebble into my hands. It was an indictment of her worth not only as a retriever but of her desire to work in deep water and the latter quality was to be exploited to the full later in her long and interesting life, but once again I run ahead of my tale.

Polly grew at an astonishing rate although I failed to appreciate just how quickly she was approaching physical maturity. Most Saturdays

Eddie would drive to my cottage and comment on what a beautiful animal Polly was becoming, although accustomed to daily contact with her as I was, I failed to notice how quickly she was maturing. It was to be a full five months before I noticed how beautiful she had become.

I arrived home early one day, exhausted with the constant confrontations with the children and irritated by the constant conflicts extant amongst the staff, only to see Polly running in the road outside my cottage. Marjorie, who cleaned my cottage when it became too dirty to be habitable, had arrived earlier and allowed Polly liberty to evacuate her bowels and bladder. Polly stood in the middle of the road, alert and beautiful, her fur shimmering in the sunlight, the embodiment of every canine grace. It is curious but German Shepherd Dogs and Siamese kittens are much like young girls. One day they are infantile and immature, scarcely attractive enough to attract attention. The next day a wonderous imago has emerged from the pupa – a creature no one could ignore and no one could fail to admire.

I sat in my car and gazed almost dumb struck at the dog standing in the lane and I believe Marjorie realised the reason for my state of

wonder. I was somewhat disappointed that Polly always let Marjorie into my cottage, greeting her as a long lost aunt each week when Marjorie called to clean, but I had long since reconciled myself to the fact Polly would never be the guard dog I desired. Yet she was scrupulously clean in the house, even on the rare occasions when I arrived home late from school, in fact, come to think, Polly never fouled in the house and my home never developed the nauseating stench of a house in which a young puppy is being kept.

Training proceeded at what best be described as a heck of a rate. I confess I am an inconsistent trainer and tend to only teach a dog an activity I enjoy – and what I enjoyed, Polly enjoyed, for she was just that sort of dog. We had long since mastered sit, lie and stay activities and Polly would stay at a sit position while I walked the three miles of road which circumnavigated the fields adjacent to my cottage. She didn't enjoy the activity (and neither did I for that matter) but she tolerated the training module patiently and greeted me joyfully when I returned. One day I learned that when I had walked around the roads, leaving Polly sitting near my cottage, a family with young children had chanced on the dog and believing Polly to be lost and distressed had tried to get her to rise and put her in the car. Polly had not risen from her stay position, and the family, believing Polly to be exhausted, had telephoned the RSPCA. I had collected Polly and gone about my day to day chores long before the RSPCA officer arrived and asked if I had seen an upset and stray husky. I know the society still performs worthwhile tasks and at one time I collected for the charity. In recent years, however, I have observed how officers are easily manipulated by those who are malicious and wish to attack a pet owner, so I refrain from even donating a penny to the organisation. Once they develop a filter system to sieve off the malicious, vindictive people who delight in reporting people they wish to cause trouble for, I shall donate to the charity once again.

Polly's ability to retrieve objects was clearly her forte, or perhaps I should be more exact and say that because I enjoy teaching dogs to retrieve, Polly entered into the activity wholeheartedly simply to please me. I began her retrieving training conventionally, rolling a crinkled piece of paper across the floor and encouraging Polly to chase the object. Once she decided to do so, I put my face near the floor and Polly came to explore my lips and mouth. Another digression I'm afraid and I beg the reader to stay with me while I explain why this technique encourages a puppy to come to the handler.

Wild dogs with puppies or cubs still residing in the lair will make a kill and bring the remains of that kill back to the lair in the most convenient carrier bag available – the bitch's stomach. When she approaches the lair the young will immediately run to the bitch and nuzzle her mouth and lips, even ignoring the teats on which they have been suckling earlier that day. This nuzzling action has the effect of causing the bitch to disgorge the contents of her stomach. The puppies now feed up on the nauseating mess vomited by the bitch, but the meat has been sanitised by the fairly strong hydrochloric acid secreted by the bitch's stomach and bone fragments are also softened by these gastric juices. The raw protein of the 'puppy meat' has also been broken down by the action of stomach pepsin and hence, to the puppies at least, the disgorged meat is highly desirable and they devour the mess with gusto.

Despite the fact that the dog has been domesticated for perhaps 12,000 years, and I believe a great deal longer, bitches still vomit the contents of their stomachs to feed puppies and, more to the point, puppies still run to the bitch's mouth to encourage her to vomit. Hence a human face is more attractive to young whelps that a human set of feet, for puppies prompted by somewhat confused race memories are wont to nuzzle human lips in an expectation of being fed. Thus people who believe that puppies are more compatible with small children than with adults are blissfully unaware that this attraction is usually due to the fact that the child's mouth, which is the main source of interest to the whelp, is nearer to the whelp's eye level than the mouth of an adult. It is interesting to note that many performing dog trainers of Medieval Europe were either dwarfs or midgets – lesson over and I shall now return to the tale of Polly and her training.

If asked which training manual has influenced my views on the training of any dog I should be forced to reply *The Dog Crusoe*, a delightfully written piece of hokum penned by Robert Michael Ballantyne, an advocate of the then very popular Newfoundland, though Ballantyne knew precious little about dogs. My first dog was trained by my attempts to emulate the skills of Dick Varley, the hero of the tale. Crusoe, the eponymous hero of the book, is taught amazing retrieving skills by his backwoodsman owner trainer and soon learns to return several miles to fetch dropped gloves, deliberately dropped by Varley. I taught my first dog these skills fairly easily, although I confess I lost many gloves during the training process! Polly's training consisted of throwing an object and praising the bitch when she brought it to hand. I would then drop the object, walk ten or so paces, turn and send the bitch to fetch the object and feign delight when she brought her 'toy' to hand. Many puppies sicken of retrieving training after three of four throws of the dummy. Polly, for reasons I have explained, somehow refused to sicken of retrieving and fetched the dummy to hand so often I believed her to be fixated with retrieving. I would sometimes hurl the object into deep nettle beds or into briars so thick that they would daunt a springer spaniel, but Polly never seemed to daunt, and eagerly awaited the next throw of the dummy.

What also amazed me was Polly's incredibly soft mouth, and for those not au fait with gundog parlance, I shall explain. Even the best bred gundogs will sometimes crush and bruise the cadaver of a bird or beast the dog is expected to retrieve. Polly was bought as a guard dog, a dog expected to protect my person or property, yet she had the softest of mouths and would retrieve an egg without cracking it. Shortly after inoculation made it possible to walk Polly off my property, she was about fifteen weeks old, she chanced on a tiny lapwing chick, a mite scarcely a day or so old, which resisted capture by crouching amongst the ploughed land opposite the house. She fetched the chick gently to hand wet but undamaged by the experience, the hen bird squawking and feigning attack on the puppy's head. Later, much later, Polly would become a formidable rabbit hunter but never once harmed a rabbit she caught.

I had discovered her affinity for water early in her life and henceforth I visited the canal regularly, if only to test her remarkable retrieving ability. However, the exercise was not without danger. After one particularly hot day tempted me to encourage her to stay in the green waters for several hours, we returned home along the lane to find Polly scouring terribly, passing a bloody, gelatinous fluid in her faeces. By the time we reached my front door she looked decidedly ill and I took her to my vet, post-haste. Richard Jones, an excellent vet and good friend, suggested that Polly had ingested some bacterium which had been harboured by the canal waters and it took many days of treatment with a broad spectrum antibiotic before she recovered from the infection. Two local youths had also swum in the canal the same day and became terribly ill as a result of an infection by the same bacteria, one youth becoming almost skeletal before the infection actually cleared.

A delightful summer slipped and slithered into a wet and stagnant autumn and Polly's training progressed at a staggering rate, never once experiencing the fits and starts one expects from any puppy. She learned a variety of skills, and for those who chose to denigrate skills to the level of tricks, I say, I pity those people. She learned to move, oh so gently, my Silky hen and her seven chicks back into the pens each night, shepherding them as gently as an aged Border collie would. Once when the hen became perplexed and upset because one chick became trapped in my thick hawthorn hedge Polly pressed through the spikes and briar stolons and retrieved the chick to hand heedless of the frenzy and impotent menace of the absurd Silkie hen who threatened a multi-toed (Silkies have an extra toe) revenge on the bitch.

The summer had been a quiet one and for some reason I escaped burglary, though two terrier puppies were taken from my run in early September. The police were less than sympathetic and the sergeant who wrote down my statement said, once again, that he was fed up with my constant burglaries. I mention that I wasn't exactly pleased about the thefts myself, but my comment was wasted on the young officer, who stormed out to record yet another undetected crime no doubt. I had long since accepted that Polly, delightful pet as she was, would never be a guard and with some trepidation awaited my next burglary. I spent some time secreting much valued objects in crevices in the house, knowing full well the police would be unable to recover them if they were stolen and that Polly would have little idea of how to protect them.

In one respect at least I was proven to be wrong – and very wrong at that.

CHAPTER 7

The Break In

Morale had sunk still further in the school in which I was teaching and discipline was at the very lowest level. I kept order in my class but avoided taking an interest in any of the events outside the classroom, avoiding the social events which might serve as a matrix to hold the crumbling life of an inner city school together. Not one of the staff now seemed to worry if the school stayed open or was closed to have its students redistributed throughout the other schools in the district. Like me, they attempted to keep order in their classes and simply hurried home at night.

On the day in question I had given three of my forty seven Godchildren in the catchment area a lift home, listened to their bleats, their discontent with the school and realised it was only a matter of time before some incident caused the powers that be to close down the establishment. I felt some despair at the hopelessness that pervaded the school, particularly as the children too realised how poor staff morale was. Our examination results were the poorest imaginable. Indeed, Walsall Observer was later to label the place 'The Worst School In The Midlands' simply because of our examination record, but it was the all-pervading sense of hopelessness which finally produced such a poor morale that the Education Authority finally decided the place should close.

I picked up a hitchhiker on the way home that day, if only to talk to someone who didn't bleat about the futility of life, but my luck was out, for the young man after unloading his backpack equipment into the car announced that he was a student teacher. His exuberance was such that I declined to enlighten him that establishments such as the school I had left existed and in order not to engage him in a conversation about schools and teachers I told him I was a greengrocery salesman and worked on a market stall. I know enough about the subject anyway, because during one of the many lows in my finances, I had helped out on such a stall. I dropped the lad on the A38 and set off along the country lanes to my cottage.

I arrived at the cottage and groaned, cradling my head in my hands, for the door of my cottage was ajar and the frame bore the unmistakable marks of a break in. I can remember shaking my head in despair, wondering how in the name of goodness could I fortify my place enough to keep these thieves out. My windows were covered in thick grid weld mesh but the door, the least fortifiable place in the home would be impossible to make secure.

I stepped inside to view the damage wrought by the burglary and, to my horror, I saw Polly, covered in blood, lying in the passage doorway. Her lovely cream fur was spattered with blood and she was obviously in great distress, yet she managed a wag of her tail to greet me. The wood panels of my cottage were smeared with blood and pools of gore stretched into the bathroom and bedrooms. One bedroom door had its hinges bruised and would shut only with some difficulty but what struck me most was the enormous quantity of blood Polly had obviously lost. I lifted her to her feet and she groaned as I did so, but despite the fact that I cleaned her fur meticulously I could find no trace of a wound through which could have seeped such a large volume of blood. I remembered one of the quotes of my boxing career that a little blood, like tea, could 'go a long way' and rechecked Polly's fur for wounds. She was obviously terribly bruised and I suspected that her ribs were broken but she had not a wound on her and her mouth indicated she was not bringing up blood from her stomach.

Quite suddenly a conclusion which would have seemed obvious to a normal person struck me like an iced towel to my face. Despite the damage wrought to Polly the blood was clearly not hers, I sprang to my feet and searched the house for the cadaver of the person who had broken into my home, but found no one, although an examination of the porch showed speckles of blood leading to a spot where my burglar had parked his car or van, and promptly rang for Eddie, my ever-present help in any trouble, before racing Polly to the vet.

Richard, the vet, eyed the badly wounded dog still pink, with a now weak solution of blood and water. I lied about the cause of the carnage partly to protect Richard who would have been required to report the incident to the police, but mostly to protect myself, as I had visions of thousands of pounds worth of damage being awarded to the miscreant who had forced his way into my premises. I resolved not to say anything, until, that is, I had spoken to Eddie.

Richard examined Polly meticulously as was his wont, but apart from a broken rib, a wrenched shoulder and considerable bruising Polly had sustained no damage which could have produced such a quantity of gore, and to my surprise Polly attempted to follow me from the vet's surgery, tottering stiffly and clearly in pain, but not suffering any serious injury.

Eddie had let himself in the house, no great feat as it was extremely difficult for me to close the door and impossible to lock it, and stood surveying the damage and gore with the air of a loss adjustor viewing damaged shipping. 'If I had to describe the scenario,' he said after assessing the overturned chairs and pools of blood, 'I'd say one or two people broke into the house and the bitch attacked them. She's eighty pounds in weight, big for a bitch, and would have given a good account of herself.' The tale of Gelert and Llewellyn's infant son flashed through my mind as Eddie spoke but I was snapped out of my reverie by Eddie, 'Personally, I'd not report this to the police. There's nothing been stolen and the damage done to the property is minimal,' he pointed at the door he was about to repair, 'If Polly has damaged anyone,' (and she obviously had) 'if the damage is serious, the police will be round in the next few days. If you report the incident, the chances are Polly will be branded a dangerous dog and life may become a little difficult. If I were you I'd wait until you get a visit from the police but I suspect that unless the victim is mortally wounded – and the human body has about 9 pints of blood,' he added, ' – you'll hear no more about the incident. I'd hate to be on the receiving side of Polly's displeasure.' he added as he repaired the lock and set the door back on its hinges again.

I lay awake that night, Polly snoring rather raucously at my bedside, and awaited reprisals for the damage Polly had wrought. No one came and the sound of the milkman rattling the crates alerted me that it was time to be readying myself for school. Polly limped painfully to her feet, tottered to the door to perform her bodily functions in the dead leaves of the woodland opposite my cottage and returned indoors to sit out the day. If I had visitors that day I really don't know, but henceforth I had no burglaries perpetrated on my property.

Eddie phoned two days later, attempting an incongruously bad impersonation of an Irish tinker, 'I hear you've got a leetle guard dog for sale, sir.' In one respect he was incorrect though, I never ever considered selling Polly.

CHAPTER 8

The Coming Of Emma

One of the advantages of working in a ghetto-type school, euphemistically referred to as an Educational Priority Area by Authorities who are usually a little embarrassed by the existence of such schools, is that I know of no teacher who teaches in such schools who suffers from insomnia. Each night I fell into a deep, black, dreamless sleep as though stunned by the tumult of the day, and each morning my alarm clock reached out through the inky blackness of my slumbers to rouse me. Sleep brings almost instant oblivion, for any teacher who wishes to preserve sanity or stay out of the coronary ward, must learn to forget the traumas of the day as soon as school finishes. Those who fail to develop interests outside school become consumed with the pettiness that makes grown men seem pitiable in the eyes of other men or, worse still, engage in a rather contemptible game, I call 'Lets Be Spiteful To Sarah' – a game involving the reluctant participation of one of the least socially adequate of the staff who is persecuted and pecked until, devoid of any self respect, the said member will literally beg a headmaster (who is often a very active participant in the game) to relocate him or her.

It is I'm afraid a fact that truly dedicated (I question this word) teachers who have no other interests other than school, who will on retirement, wane and fade into some incurable malaise and die. I believe that the decline is due in part to the fact that such teachers are social vampires who actually need to see the stress and misery of their colleagues and, deprived of such spiritual nourishment, such teachers slip and slither into nothingness and die. James Hilton knew nothing of comprehensive education and his ever-innocent, benign Mr Chips figure is noticeable by his absence in most modern schools. I've waxed lyrical for too long – now on with my tale.

I was awoken on Saturday morning by the ringing of my telephone. A man with one of those rather slick cosmopolitan accents (which immediately make me feel inferior) spoke without bothering to introduce himself, 'Are you Brian Plummer?' (and without waiting to confirm whether or not I was), 'I understand you are able to train pigs,' – and once again without waiting for a reply – 'We need a trained pig for an Italian film about a woman called,' he paused a second, to check his notes, no doubt, 'Lady Jane Gordon.' I knew of the lady, a rather brazen hussy whose only claim to fame was that she had once ridden a pig through the streets of Edinburgh – a rather harmless if rather ridiculous gesture of her individuality, I thought. I mentioned I knew of the lady and the speaker at the other end of the telephone became elated, 'Great, great,' he enthused and mentioned a sum of money which made the futility of my 9–4 lifestyle all too apparent. 'Could you do it?' he concluded – mentioning no act in particular.

Now, at times, I am fairly convinced that I have multiple personality problems, for quite suddenly I heard someone speaking in my voice reply, 'Yes, of course, I've trained lots of pigs,' and was snapped back to reality by the agent/producer who quite excitedly began speaking of such things as contracts, deadlines, liaisons with directors and a host of other baffling subjects about which I haven't the slightest idea.

'You'll be 'anged by your tongue,' said Moses who arrived some ten or so minutes later and was making tea while I sat, still in my pyjamas, relating the tale of the morning telephone call. Moses was a settled Romany, considerably brighter than I was and perhaps the most worldly person I have ever met. 'You know nuffin' of pigs, so what possessed you to say you could train one?' I countered with the comment that I'd trained hundreds of pigs during my teaching years, but the allusion was wasted on Mo as he continued, 'It's like with the bloody women. Yer in over yer head before you can say Jack Robinson. I dunno'. He shook his head sagely, bewildered by the stupidity I had displayed by accepting the contract to train a pig. I miss Mo dreadfully these days. He seldom said much, and many of his epigrams were garnished with four letter words, but he was the wisest of men. 'There's more rhyme or reason in yer dog,' he explained, gesturing at Polly as he did so and stormed into the kitchen to pour my tea, cursing as he did, lamenting the day he had ever met me, no doubt.

Come to think of it, Mo was absolutely right, for at this stage of my life I knew nothing of pigs and things porcine. I'd experienced close encounters of the worst kind as a child when I had attempted to run across Owen Phillips' allotment which held a giant, gaunt Tamworth boar, kept razor thin by dint of worms and wartime feeding rationing, but the encounter had done little to endear me to pigs. Later in college my translation of the Greek tale *The Boar Hunt Of Calydon* did, if anything, warn me to be careful of pigs or anything piglike when I read an all to graphic account of how a wild pig had managed to castrate Ancaeus, one of the hunters who had attempted to hunt the beast, an accident which gave an entirely different meaning to the expression 'tragic hero', I thought at the time, but I was jarred out of my reverie by Moses' raucous cry of, 'They'll be writing a book about you and yer bleedin' pigs and calling it *All Creatures Grunt And Smell*,' as he closed my front door and spat contemptuously in the corner of my porch. 'Weird, you are! Weird,' he shouted as he stormed to his car and drove off towards Lichfield.

Polly adored Mo, and while she became suspicious, and even hostile, if anyone so much as raised his voice to me, she tolerated Mo's rantings and ravings with a wag of the tail. She had a curious perspicacity where people were concerned and as she aged and I began to mature, I learned to respect her judgement concerning people. If she tolerated a stranger or greeted him cordially, I learned the stranger meant me no harm. If she avoided contact or disdained a stranger's advances, I became suspicious of the person's intentions. She allowed Eddie and Mo in and out of the house whenever the pair wished to visit me and always greeted them joyfully, but met scrap collectors, or those combing the country cottages for antiques, with a fury that amazed me. I can't explain her attitude. Maybe my own moods and fears were captured by the dog and she responded accordingly. She allowed infants from the local village to plunder my orchard with impunity. Conversely, she downed a tinker who, uninvited, had decided to investigate the scaffolding below the pear trees. I can still remember his terrified face staring up at me and his mouth stammering, 'Are you selling dese scaffold poles, sir?', but I am wandering and losing my tale yet again.

Monday morning, a contract and a pile of impedimenta I have learned to associate with film making, arrived in the post, and as I sat in front of the fire dressing and drinking my tea – a curious set of movements which have attracted considerable attention – I became aware of the fine mess into which I had stepped because of my total ignorance of pigs and all things porcine. I was required, by contract, to not only 'gentle the pig' (I'm still wondering what this expression actually means) and to have the creature saddle broken and obedient to its rider's commands. Matters were made considerably worse by the presence of an advance that assured me my electric bill would be paid for at least the next quarter. If I had been a brave man, or for that matter an honourable man, I would have returned the cheque post-haste stating that I would be unable to fulfil the contract. As it is, I am neither honourable nor brave, and so I cashed the cheque immediately and waded deeper and deeper into the mire of deception.

I drove to school that morning with my mind filled with thoughts of pigs and things porcine, and to my great pleasure I realised I knew a lot of the theoretical aspects of pig husbandry and pigs in general. I had long since realised that pigs were a lot more intelligent and perhaps sensitive than the swill gobbling, filth wading creatures people believed them to be – and come to think of it, man has savagely abused the pig, like just about every other animal he has sought to domesticate.

Pigs were regarded as unclean by the Torah and the Koran, holy books of the Jews and Muslims, not because of the habits of pigs but simply because primitive swine refused to be herded and were thus regarded as symbols of the lifestyle of settled peoples, which the nomadic Jews and Arabs found abhorrent and unacceptable. The fact that Middle Eastern pigs sometimes carried trichinosis, a curious and fatal disease, was not understood by the nomadic people, for the disease would not manifest itself for many months after the meal of undercooked pork.

French farmers often used heavily muzzled pigs to seek for truffles – a fungus with edible subterraneous fruiting bodies – and the pigs gleefully rooted up the truffles although their muzzle prevented them eating the fungi. However, as the truffle finding pigs became larger their frustration concerning the denial of truffles they had rooted out made them difficult to handle and hence it became expedient to train a somewhat smaller, more manageable truffle hunting swine each year.

On the subject of the hunting qualities of pigs, there is the tale of the HPR (hunt, point, retrieve) pig of Georgian days, which not only put pointers to shame finding pheasants and partridge but stood point as well as any setter until the birds were flushed and shot. The pig then ran into cover and retrieved the cadaver to hand as gently as would any retriever. Now I had always been just a little sceptical about the tale, particularly as pigs will snatch and gobble up farmyard fowl which had the temerity to approach a feeding pig, but the tale of the pig, which, bore the somewhat unseemly appellation 'Slut', is recorded in most books concerning farmyard beasts.

As I approached Muckley Corner (rather aptly named considering the subject), my mind flashed to a statement made by Havelock Ellis. who had a penchant for rather murky sexual tales, that the pig was the most commonly sexually abused of all farmyard animals. Not that such tales concerned me, I must add, for at that time at least I led a fairly hectic social life. Indeed there are some quite unpleasant stories concerning the behaviour of pigs. In the Middle Ages pigs which offended by eating children, or by being the object of some lunatic's sexual desires, were tried in a most official fashion, automatically found guilty and promptly committed to the flames – a fairly common Medieval method of removing any undesirable or antisocial activity it seems.

Early man, once he had passed through the hunter-gatherer and nomadic herdsman lifestyle and became a settled dweller, started to domesticate the wild pig and then, true to form, killed off the wild relatives of the farmyard swine. However he tended to ignore domesticating the European wild boar which is a fearsome creature – 'and where he strikes his crooked tushes slay,' – as Shakespeare so aptly puts it, and chose the Indian pig Sus Vitatus as the ancestor of the porkers and baconers of today, but it would only be a matter of time before the pig entered into the idiom of most European and Asian languages.

The biblical quote, 'Casting pearls before swine' is possibly a translator's error. T. H. White – at the risk of name dropping, I knew him quite well – believed that translators mixed up margarite (a pearl) with marguerite, a type of daisy, and hence the expression should have read 'attempting to feed pigs on daisies' – a total waste of flowers.

While still on the subject of the scriptures and things biblical, it is a fact that pigs have a small hole in their forefeet which is only discernible after the bristle is removed. The ancients believed demons entered via such apertures and hence pigs were ready victims of demonic possession. The tale of the Gaderene swine indicates just how easily pigs could be possessed by a legion of demons, although I must confess I have always wondered if the owner of the Gaderene swine recovered any compensation for the death of his livelihood.

On the subject of pigs conveying people – to have the beast saddle broken – the expression piggyback comes readily to mind. However, such an expression has little to do with pigs and is derived from the Italian *pigar*, a child, for women, before the invention of prams, were once wont to carry children piggyback.

More interesting still is the expression 'buying a pig in a poke'. Now it appears that Medieval fairs were dens of iniquity and havens for cheats and rogues. Young piglets, swine which differed little from wild pigs, were taken to market in sacks and because young pigs were such escapists the potential buyer was encouraged to feel the piglet rather than peer into the bag to view it. Other unscrupulous sellers often replaced the pig with an adult cat – similar in shape and weight to a half-wild, primitive eight-week-old piglet. Hence when the buyer arrived home he promptly 'let the cat out of the bag'.

Yet the truth was that I knew little of the physical properties of pigs and less still of how to harness one to allow an actress to ride the creature, and at this point the fact that I had not only accepted but spent the advance struck like a thunderbolt. My dreamless sleep, the result of total exhaustion, was now punctuated with dreams of portly CID officers interviewing me and spelling advance incorrectly on the statement they were writing. One of the CID officers coughed, swore and picked his nose before returning to a fearsomely badly written statement – indeed it was a fairly realistic type of dream!

The following week a school half-day allowed me a chance to pop Polly into my van and visit Lichfield market. After trampling through floods of animal excrement I arrived at the pig pens to watch the sale of baconers and porkers, for I was already becoming au fait with the terms associated with pig production. As I watched, I became acutely aware that the legend that man allowed animals to trade the hardship of freedom for the comforts of domestication were so terribly wrong, for pigs are appallingly treated by those who own or trade in 'on the trotter pork'. The pigs destined for slaughter were marked – a delicious euphemism by any standards – by puncturing the fleshy ears with a huge punch, whereupon the wretched beasts screamed, shook their heads and showered blood onto the ghouls watching the spectacle.

I could not resist voicing my disgust at the barbarism I was witnessing – quietly of course for I have never been a brave man – but my whispered criticism was picked up by one of the onlookers – one Graham Stephens, and there began a fortuitous and lasting relationship. I was in the act of removing the specks of blood which were staining Polly's creamy-white coat when an onlooker spoke. 'There's no real need for this,' – he gestured to the spectacle of bloodstained, frightened pigs – 'you know,' he said, and promptly introduced himself to me. My associate had been a lecturer in an agricultural college and his specialist subject had been – yes, you've guessed it – pigs! It was a fortuitous encounter for through Graham the world of pigs began to open like a rather disgusting, smelly painted fan.

Graham began his first lecture – *Pigs Aren't What They Used To Be* – and thereby prevented me from making an ass of myself by attempting to train a modern commercial large white type pig. The modern white porker is, in fact, a far cry from the red or reddish-grey swine kept by farmers and householders alike during the times when Lady Jane Gordon roamed the streets of Edinburgh mounted on her pig.

The fat, fast growing, meal gobbling pigs of today have in fact resulted from ameliorating the acorn grubbing, mast feeding native swine with blubbery Chinese pigs, the sort that river people kept aboard junks and fed on household waste and fish. The combination of the two distinct types produced the modern commercial pigs which fattened to killing weight in a mere six months, whereas the razor-backed native British pigs were still growing at two years of age.

Graham explained that the type of pig found in Scotland during Lady Jane's time was long extinct but relics of this past age might still be found in rare breeds parks or private collections kept by those who liked to see a pig in its natural setting, foraging and grubbing in fields rather than waxing fat in cages and denied natural light. In such natural conditions ancient breeds of pig could scarcely be profitable but the dedication of those few who sought to preserve ancient breeds allowed such antique varieties to survive. Each year the numbers of these rare breeds shrank a little more yet those who sought to preserve these strange looking pigs continued to produce more piglets to allow these breeds to survive.

I visited Hensons rare breed park in the Cotswolds and after much deliberation decided that I must purchase a piglet from a Berkshire sow – a jet black roly poly type pig, glutinously fat but tough enough to support the weight of an actress – and docile enough to allow the woman to ride the pig. Moses had, after much disdain for the piglet, sneered that a copper-red Tamworth would fit the bill, for Moses after much persuasion, 'confessed' that he had worked with pigs and knew a great deal about them. Tamworths were, according to Moses, tough enough to survive my mistakes in feeding and docile enough to handle, although Mo still sneered at the nature of my project and condemned my dishonesty in accepting and spending my advance. 'How you gonna pay the money back when yer fail to train the pig? ' he sneered, 'Yer afraid of horses, so how yer gonna saddle break a pig? Go on, tell me,' he chided angrily. Mo had hit the nail on the head regarding my fear of things equine – for like Cole Porter, I felt the French had the right idea about horses, they ate them.

As it was, I bought neither Berkshire or Tamworth, nor, might I add, the very primitive, but scarcely true breeding Oxfordshire Black and Sandy, though this variety of pig is not only attractive but fairly typical of eighteenth and nineteenth century pigs. By the merest of chance I dropped in on a one time neighbour, one Terry Woodward, who was in charge of an experimental project which specialised in producing chestnut-red coloured giant pigs called Durocs, which while the breed produced boars which were often fierce and treacherous, the sows were often the most meek and gentle of animals. What was even better, was that despite the enormous size to which the sows grew, they resembled some of the primitive pigs which would have produced mounts for the incorrigible Lady Jane Gordon. Better still, the Duroc had been named after a winning racehorse so the coincidence augured well.

Terry heard my tale, and, without further ado, began adopting a small red piglet from a litter which had recently been born on the experimental unit. Emma, as I later called the piglet was allowed to suckle her mother to obtain the vital antibody saturated colostrum which would protect her against disease in later life, but was socialised by being taken into the house to play with Terry's family and, what was more important, Terry's Border terrier puppy. Thus, by the time I collected Emma she was extraordinarily tame and, alas, had absolutely no fear of terriers – and this was almost to be her downfall, I'm afraid – but once again I run ahead of my tale.

I had half expected some problems concerning Emma's behaviour, for animals separated from their own kind during the critical period of their development often behave atypically later in life. The German word *Prägnung*, translated rather unfaithfully as imprinting, can often explain curious behaviour in certain animals and birds. It was once the custom for New York flat dwellers to take on young dog and bitch puppies at an age when the whelps should have been suckling their dams. Such dogs grew up with an almost obsessive devotion to their owners which clearly delighted the flat dwellers. However these dogs were often distressed when they encountered their own kind and when their owners decided to breed from their animals, the males were often baffled by the flirtatious courtship ritual of in-season bitches, and flat reared bitches were terrified when an amorous normal male dog attempted to mate them. Indeed it appears that while mammals have a great deal of instinctive behaviour to steer them through life, much of what is considered to be normal behaviour needs to be learned.

Emma was a joyful piglet who had played happily with Terry's Border terrier puppy, engaging it in wild games, wrestling and nosing in the curious manner nestling piglets display. When she arrived at my house Polly accepted Emma patiently, stoically, tolerating her advances as the piglet leaped on her and raced over the reclining bitch's sides and back, her sharp pink hooves obviously causing the dog some pain. On Emma's arrival Polly had glanced at me as if seeking instructions as to what to do, failed to detect any trace of concern in my manner and blindly and unquestioningly accepted the pig's position in the household.

The other dogs regarded Emma with some suspicion. Vampire, who was greeted with an effusive display of affection by the piglet, snarled slightly and tried to avoid the animal henceforth. Omega, his daughter, disdainfully ignored Emma's advances and henceforth kept well away from the piglet. Pagan, however, displayed an implacable hatred of the animal, her face assuming a wild, excited expression whenever the piglet appeared and, try as I might, I could not bring Pagan to accept the presence of the infant animal. Pagan's eyes took on a glazed expression whenever Emma appeared and the terrier's body quivered with an almost obscene excitement. It was almost inevitable what was to follow, but despite my claims of stockmanship and a knowledge of animal behaviour, I failed to notice what would have been patently obvious to even the casual observer.

Emma had been allotted the lower portion of my lengthy garden and allowed to roam free. When I arrived home I shouted her name and excitedly she scaled the galvanised fence and raced to greet me, her tiny hooves clattering on the tarmac. She would follow me into the house, greet Polly as a long lost friend while Polly wagged her tail and patiently accepted Emma's somewhat painful caresses. Emma was meticulously clean in the house and simply barged at the door when nature called, urging me to allow her access to the deep bed of oak leaves at the bottom of the garden. However, to reach the house and arrive at the oak leaf bed, Emma had to pass in front of Pagan's pen and Pagan became as though demented whenever the piglet passed.

Now, with hindsight, I could have predicted the catastrophe and possibly taken steps to prevent it, but I have seldom been gifted with seer sight and each day brought the inevitable disaster closer to hand.

I arrived home that day, slammed my car door and shouted 'Emma' and waited for the inevitable clatter of tiny feet, but Emma didn't appear. Puzzled, I strode down the path to see Pagan excitedly shaking what I believed to be a muddy sack, but on closer examination I realised the 'bag' sported an eye that blinked and closed from time to time. I beat Pagan off the terribly damaged piglet only to find her leaping up at me as I cradled Emma in my arms. Twice Pagan leapt, missed a hold and, in her frenzy, sank her teeth into my arm. Finally I managed to catch the crazed animal and kennelled her but by this time the eye emerging from the bag of mud had closed, for Emma was unconscious.

I raced to the house and filled a bowl with warm water and salt and attempted to bathe Emma, but the wounds I uncovered were fearsome. Emma opened her eyes at one stage, screamed slightly, and then mercifully fell unconscious again as I bathed, cleaned and disinfected her horrible rips and punctures, but I found it impossible not to wince when I realised the damage Pagan had wrought on the six week old piglet.

Polly strolled around, inspecting the damage perhaps, and curious about the immobility of the once joyful and frisky piglet. I cleaned Emma thoroughly and wrapped her in a blanket and promptly lit a fire, for pneumonia as much as septic poisoning is likely to carry off a badly wounded animal. Polly was intrigued by the activity and carefully cleaned the frothy spume that appeared on Emma's snout but the piglet showed little other signs of life.

In despair I sat on my rocking chair, head in hands, the only panacea I knew to attempt to rectify some disaster. I had but eight months not only to rear my piglet but to break her to the saddle and gentle her enough to allow a somewhat apprehensive person to ride a pig, and now my piglet had clearly come to an abrupt halt. It would, I suppose, be possible to obtain another piglet from Terry, but Emma had become a part of the household and would be impossible to replace.

I gazed at the fat, tiny piglet lying swathed in towels and cursed Pagan and her frenzied desire to kill just about every creature she encountered. As evening fell Emma was still only semi-concious and her future looked very bleak indeed. Polly too seemed affected by Emma's plight and from time to time she rose from her place next to my chair to sniff and examine the stricken creature.

I built up the fires and prepared to sit out the night as I had done so many times with injured animals. I rocked to and fro in my chair like a near catatonic who had rejected the world and all its problems. The telephone rang and some woman, I forget her name, bleated that she was waiting to be picked up and taken to the theatre. I made some trite excuse for my absence – a blatant lie I'm afraid – for the excuse of sitting with an injured and dying piglet seemed a shade too ludicrous to relate. The lady listened as I lied and lied again then replaced the receiver, totally unaware of the misery and gloom that permeated my home that night.

I returned to the room where Emma was lying still swathed in towels and noticed that the piglet had opened her eyes and Polly was eagerly cleaning the bloodstained spume that was seeping from Emma's torn nostrils. Delighted with Emma's improvement I decided to sit with her until dawn.

It is only when some dire accident slows down the pace of my life to a moderate gallop that I become aware of the lifestyle of my fellow man. I lived life at a furious rate, hunting my terrier pack as much as five nights a week and seldom staying at home for the evening. I had often wished I had time to watch some of the television programmes discussed so eagerly by the school staff each morning and felt decidedly out of the swing of things when I confessed I was not au fait with certain series.

Now with an evening to spare I became aware of how trite, banal and mundane most people's lives are and I am amazed at the absolute rubbish watched by the average viewer who has not the strength of will to switch off the infernal machine and do something constructive. One programme centred on the plight of unmarried lesbian mothers living in damp houses in Bradford; I switched over, only to see a programme concerned with student life in Taiwan – which seemed little different from student life in Sheffield. A third channel featured a game show with a theme so bewildering that I failed to follow the intricate scoring system as the quiz master sought to deliberately humiliate the contestants. I watched a while, became totally baffled and then switched to the fourth channel just in time to see how some obscene tropical worms had infested a toothless Mexican woman's legs. Do the powers that be consider such programmes interesting and edifying? Do people actually race home and look forward to see some strange worm destroy people? I switched off and sat back in my chair and thanking God I hadn't bothered to buy a television licence.

The heat and humidity in the house made me sleepy and I began to doze fitfully, from time to time glancing at the blanket-beswathed piglet and at Polly who lay near my chair gazing at the injured infant pig. The constant spume appearing on Emma's muzzle intrigued the bitch and periodically she would rise and carefully approach the piglet, staring at the beast intently before she cleaned the blood-speckled froth from Emma's nostrils. Polly was clearly fascinated by the wounded piglet but I had some doubts about her motives regarding the creature. Stricken animals attract the attention of predators, and despite many thousands of years of domestication Polly was, despite her tractable, gentle nature, essentially a predator.

As the clock ticked its way to midnight my telephone rang repeatedly. I am fairly certain that once the pubs close for the night the typical inadequates' minds lightly turn to thoughts of lurchers. Every night I stayed in I was treated to enquiries as to how some drunken lout could obtains some bizarrely bred lurcher composite and apparently I am not alone in experiencing such midnight lurcher enquiries. It is amazing just how many coursing enthusiasts only seem to come to life after closing time and wander abroad attempting to annoy people. To deal with such telephone pests I have devised a series of epigrams such as 'Keep taking the tablets mate' or 'Does your psychiatrist realise you are using the telephone?' or 'How do you manage to dial from the cosy confines of your straight jacket?'. I doubt if such comments ever go home , so to speak, for the demented creatures on the other end are usually too numbed by drink to be hurt by comments I consider to be clever. Truly there are some strange people in this world – and the majority of them have an interest in dogs!

Sleep eventually prevailed, despite my determination to keep awake. At 3.00am I awoke sharply and stared across the room to see Emma's bloodstained towels devoid of Emma. A split second panic overwhelmed me and in moments I had scripted a half dozen different scenarios. Had Emma crawled away to find some distant place to die, for many animals display a preference for dying in private. Had Polly found the dead piglet, carried it off and was perhaps at this very moment dining on Emma's tiny corpse?

I rose shakily, still numbed by the heat and humidity within the house. Polly was nowhere to be seen and this confirmed my worst suspicions. However, I ran through the house calling Polly's name if only to assure myself of Emma's grisly fate.

I found Polly in the kitchen, pressed against the sink unit and for a moment noticed only her bloodstained jowls. I groaned aloud and wondered what punishment would be suitable and appropriate for a dog that had killed and eaten a piglet. Only then did I notice the tiny piglet suckling Polly, noisily nuzzling at the bitch's teats and to my amazement obviously obtaining some sustenance for her efforts. Polly had experienced a phantom pregnancy only a week previous, for she was essentially an Earth Mother, and adopted all the signs of pregnancy after each and every season. I sat on the chair amazed by the spectacle and had to restrain myself from telephoning Eddie or David to come and see the phenomenon.

Actually interspecies adoptions are far from uncommon and there is scarcely a country dweller who has not heard of someone whose cat had adopted a squirrel or a rabbit or kitten. There is a tale of a Midland travelling menagerie which had a ratling running amongst a nest of ferret kittens and both ferrets and ratling setting about and killing any strange rats which were tipped into the cage. There is the tale of Romulus and

Remus, the builders of Rome, who were adopted by a she-wolf, and if the tale seems a little fanciful, there is a well documented account of how the Reverend Singh found a pair of young girls, Amala and Kamala, amongst a nest of wolves.

The adoption process is usually roughly the same. The foster mother must obviously be ready to adopt strange creatures before the first interspecies encounter takes place. The fosterling creature must then manifest an appearance or emit sounds which trigger the adoption response – for instance a plaintive cry and the foster mother must respond to the stimulus. Just recently one of my terriers, a bitch which at one time detested cats, found a tiny day old kitten in the hedgerow. Cats have a habit of abandoning a nest once the lair has been discovered or disturbed and the day previous a noisy family of children had discovered the tiny kittens under some rubbish. Pippin, my terrier bitch, found the kitten and for some reason brought it home and promptly came into milk to suckle the creature. The kitten grew up totally unafraid of dogs but decidedly curious and hesitant about cats. It will be interesting to see if this queen will mate with a tom and how she behaves towards her own kittens – but once again I am digressing.

Over the next few days friends and strangers arrived to see and photograph the strange sight of a dog suckling a piglet and it would be fair to say that Emma's training began from this time forth. Polly meticulously cleaned the gaping rips wrought by Pagan and slowly the piglet recovered from the onslaught. In days she accompanied Polly and myself on walks across the fields and came to hand as obediently as any gundog when called.

I had hitherto marvelled and questioned the retrieving ability of the pig Slut. Now as I proceeded to train Emma, I realised that pigs are quite eager to retrieve objects to hand, particularly if the pig is well socialised as a piglet. Emma after a start at retrieving a rolled up ball of paper, lumbered after Frisbees, sometimes retrieving them with a rush which took me off my feet. Yet even when Emma reached a huge 300lb in weight, a giant, excitable, gently glutinous blob of a pig, she still suckled Polly.

Emma was broken to the saddle with contemptuous ease and seemed to delight in having a small person on her back but when the time came for her to perform, the actress glanced at Emma, mistook the pig's glee at seeing her for savagery and then allowed an understudy to perform in her place. My eighteen months of training my giant pig was reduced to a five second blurred shot, deliberately distorted to protect the identity of the rider. Still, that's show business I suppose.

I am reluctant to leave a tale partially told. Emma, huge and glutinous as she was, desired motherhood and was sent to be mated by an enormous large white boar. During the act of mating the couple fell and the action broke Emma's back. I do so wish that at least some of my tales had a happy ending!

CHAPTER 9

Cottage In
The Highlands

It is said that no one ever forgets one's army pay book number and despite the fact that I concluded my somewhat inglorious national service in 1957, I can still recall that impersonalised army number. Likewise, no one ever forgets the date of one's first coronary, one's first dice with death so to speak – in my case June 5th 1985, but again I run ahead of my tale.

In January 1983 I had saved a large sum of money, or to be more precise the largest sum of money ever to grace my bank account, nearly £2,000, and the money burned in my pocket. Polly had been mated to her grandfather, a huge yellow dog which carried a variety of genetic defects that were to be the downfall of my kennels in later years. Her children Bimbo and Felicity were perhaps the best looking bitches I have ever seen and as a monumental error of judgement, I inbred to them. My Lichfield kennel was full to overflowing and for the first time in my life I felt financially secure. I have often stated that at that time in my life Paul Getty was not the richest man in the world for it was I who deserved that appellation. Getty wanted more, whereas I had everything I desired!

Some months before, I had had a windfall at the card tables, a night when Lady Luck spurned everyone but me and for once in my rather spendthrift life I was able to walk away from the tables cash in hand. My eleven hundred pounds literally burned my pocket, for I was reluctant to put the money in the bank lest the Inland Revenue questioned where and how I had obtained such a sum. Hence, I devised ways of carrying

the money around with me.

My burglaries had ceased, for I believe Polly had deterred the villains who had pillaged my property – for tales of a savage dog (how inaccurate that expression was) soon gets around the criminal classes. Yet I felt that the act of secreting £1,100 in cash around my premises was virtually inviting a break in, so rather foolishly I carried around the money wherever I went. Hitherto I had regarded the mental picture of Silas Marner crooning and drooling over his secret cache of money as a figment of the imagination of the writer George Elliot. Now I believe that the authoress had made a careful study of misers and had had ample opportunity to observe the affectations of those who hoard money.

Each night I arrived home and counted my wad, never daring to spend a penny of my ill gotten gains lest I broke into my capital. One evening as I was counting the money I glanced up and observed a cyclist gazing the windows of my cottage with an astonished look on his face. The chances are that the poor fellow had no evil intentions but his presence strengthened my resolve to carry the money with me wherever I went, and now began my financial dilemma.

I taught in a ghetto where muggings were by no means uncommon and the £1,100 would have seemed like a windfall to any ne'er do well out to make a few pounds by dint of a quick head butt or a dextrous knee to the groin. Muggers seldom bother to thoroughly search a victim they have downed and usually simply snatch a wallet before haring off to spend the loot. Hence, the first thing next day I changed my £1,100 into fifty pound notes and secreted my swag in my shoes, an action which gave my ambling gait a certain Jacques Tatti-like movement, and which would certainly attracted the attentions of a mugger, or for that matter a casual onlooker. Therefore the very next day I changed my twenty two fifty pound notes for eleven one hundred pound notes which allowed me to walk a little more freely.

I cannot remember who said it, and I'm too lazy to look it up, but apparently one only sees the things one perceives. Hence anyone who has installed a Sky reception disc notices similar discs wherever he or she gazes. Likewise, a Dalmatian owner's life soon becomes filled with spotted dogs. My own particular predicament was exacerbated by the fact that wherever I looked I saw references to muggers and the deeds such social undesirables perform. A newspaper casually thrown on the staff room table immediately fell open at an article about a woman who had been attacked and robbed of her life savings. Likewise, all television channels seemed to be running series concerning armed robberies and muggers, so the following week, spurred on by my paranoia, I went yet again to the bank to change my £1,100 notes to notes of smaller denominations. I must also admit that, after this visit to the bank, the tellers nudged each other whenever I appeared. My theory was this. If a mugger found some money in my jacket they would, like as not, run off not thinking to check my shoes, whereas if they found nothing on my person the chances are they would search my person thoroughly to make the mugging worthwhile. However notes of small denominations secreted in various places about my person needed to be counted regularly and hence the plot thickened, so to speak.

Each day, shortly after work, I would go for tea in one of the Walsall cafes and after tea seek out a toilet in which to check and count my £1,100. Now Walsall is fairly unique in having what public prosecutors refer to as 'notorious toilets', I'll explain what I mean presently. That particular day I went into a cubicle, carefully locked the door and began taking off various items of my apparel to count my money. As I did so to my utter amazement I noticed a mirror attached to a length of stick being pushed under the partition from the next cubicle (it takes all sorts to make a world – or so it appears).

With a sudden rush of courage I snatched up the mirror and dashed out of the cubicle still holding the mirror and stick, only to find a man, clad in a long Macintosh, running from the next cubicle out to the main street.

A heavily built labourer who was in the process of using the latrine noticed the mirror in my hand, the figure of the Macintosh pervert fleeing into the street and drew entirely the wrong conclusion from the scenario. 'You bloody weirdo,' he stormed, 'Yer need to be stopped. Bloody gelded, if yer asks me. Yer nutters, everyone', he uttered, nodding at a particularly vivid piece of graffiti which described some man's unnatural desire for hats, handbags and his elderly aunt. It would have been futile to stop and explain that I had visited the toilet to count my money and who the real pervert was – so I slunk out and tried to mingle in the crowded shopping centre, finally going into W. H. Smiths where standing next to the magazine stall I noticed an article concerning *Perverts And Public Lavatories* – I've just remembered, it was William James who made that statement about perception.

I arrived home, shaken by my experiences, and realised the stupidity of carrying my ill gotten gains on my person. Eddie telephoned later that evening and suggested I put my money into bricks and mortar rather than tempting yet another incident in the toilet. So the very next day I sent off for brochures for isolated properties, though not before visiting the bank, changing my £1 notes into 50p pieces and secreting them in the space behind the skirting boards!

I had always fancied buying a country cottage in Scotland, partly because I knew and liked Scotland and partly because of the fire hazard a Welsh holiday cottage presented once misguided fanatics realised that I had blood other that of a pure Celtic variety in my veins. Hence I wrote to Scottish estate agents and solicitors for brochures, for I was blissfully unaware that while it is extremely easy to buy a cottage in Scotland, it is extremely difficult to sell one. The brochures arrived by the sackful convincing me that a new Highland Clearance was now in progress, for in districts with a high unemployment rate country cottages were readily available.

A curious attitude towards strangers exists in the Highlands and to a certain extent in Wales. It is argued that English buyers are purchasing all the available properties leaving ghost villages in winter months, these villages only coming to life during the summer holidays. Nationalist zealots are of the belief that such properties should be sold for a song to locals, though these cottages are not so numerous that they are easily available to any local boy who wishes to buy one. This nationalistic notion is further compounded by the belief that Highlanders and cottage-firing Welsh fanatics believe that while a Celtic bricklayer may earn £200 a week, an English bricklayer is fetching home his wages in a giant sack. The fact that unions usually insist that there is a degree of financial parity in certain trades throughout Britain is often overlooked. Highlanders seem convinced that they have only to cross the borders to find a land flowing with milk and honey, albeit English milk and honey. No Highlander believes that there is poverty anywhere else in Britain and is totally unaware of the hideous squalor and malnourishment which occurs in some of the inner cities. Every Englishman is a Rothschild, every English artisan is a grossly overpaid capitalist and every Highlander a deprived Celt, sneered at by the wealthy English tourist and kept in abject poverty by the guile of the current government. It is useless to attempt to explain to Highlanders that teachers are underpaid in both Scotland and England and that most tradesmen are paid a standard rate for their services whether they work in Thurso or Tavistock, for such Highlanders are convinced they are having a raw deal from life. It is also useless to explain to such people that it is Scottish landlords who are benefiting by selling these cottages to outsiders, for zealots are set in their ways and refuse to listen to logic or heed statistics. The English are rich and the Scots are not, is the only dictum these fanatics will heed. Still there are a great many serviceable cottages available in the Highlands simply because lack of local employment has drastically reduced the number of house-buying Scots who may want to purchase these cottages.

However, politics and economics aside, I finally settled on a brochure for a newly renovated croft house with three and a half acres of land at the most northerly portion of the British mainland. Caithness is a curious county in as much as while it is classed a part of the Highlands, it is in fact virtually as flat as Norfolk. Bordered on two sides by some of the wildest seas in the world, the county has far more arable land than the rest of the Northern Highlands and hence land is more expensive than in Sutherland. However, some twenty years ago, when I bought my Highland cottage, property was incredibly cheap in Caithness and this fact attracted me to the brochure sent me by the estate agents.

These days Caithness has an unsavoury reputation for being a county of dropouts, social misfits with no means of support and with no ambitions of ever seeking employment of any sort. I suppose that in many ways this reputation is justified, for if one is unemployed there is no better place to live than in Caithness. Life proceeds at a leisurely rate. Indeed there is no Caithnessian expression that has the imperative nature of the word *mañana*. The locals complain that social derelicts are invading the county and occupying all the farm cottages and that the crime rate within the county has risen accordingly, but this was not always the case.

Some twenty years ago, when I first considered buying a Caithnessian cottage, the country was delightfully parochial and apart from a fierce hatred of all things English (and anyone south of Perth was considered to be English) the Caithnessian was indifferent to the events occurring in the outside world. Indeed an explosion of an atomic bomb rendering the city of London a smouldering ruin would have less effect on a Caithnessian than the drop in the wholesale price of live crabs that such an attack might produce. The Caithnessian is deliciously nosy and that is, if anything, a massive understatement. It is commonly believed that few Caithnessian households do not have a pair of binoculars in the window seats and people-watching takes on a whole new meaning north of Inverness.

There is a tale, which is obviously apocryphal, about a German spy who during the dark days of World War II was parachuted onto the coastline of Caithness and ordered to contact a spy called MacKay. Now anyone who has visited the Highlands will be aware that one in every two Highlanders appear to be called MacKay. So the bewildered and perplexed spy decides to knock on the door of the first MacKay household he encounters and utter the password in the hopes that his contact will be identified. He knocks on the front door and as soon as the householder appears the spy splutters, 'The green rat rides at midnight'. The householder is not the least perplexed and answers, 'No, I am MacKay the postman, MacKay the spy is at the croft on the next bend'.

Yet the spacious nature of Caithness, and the total freedom this wilderness seems to exude, is bound to attract southerners who are silently rebelling against the cramped conditions which are all too common in the south. There's a tale of an US judge, slack-mouthed and uncouth as only southern American judges are allowed to be, who once said that if he couldn't take a 'leak' outside his front porch without someone seeing him urinate, it was time to move further from town. Such a judge would find Caithness an ideal land in which to live.

Yet of course such an idyllic land also attracts those who wish to opt out of society while retaining the social perks society has to offer. In fact, the Caithnessian may well be correct in thinking that the county has absorbed a host of social misfits from both Scotland and England! Such misfits have little desire to work and, since their arrival, the crime rate within the county has certainly increased dramatically. At one time it was considered something short of sacrilege to steal creels or fishing equipment from boats and harbours. No one ever even considered stealing peat that was stacked by the roadside and left until it had dried enough to be collected and hauled home. Alas, this is not the case today, but I have eulogised too long on the merits of solitude and lamented the increase of undesirables a shade too much.

Scotland has some curious yet very sensible rules and regulations, the most sensible of which are the laws concerning the purchase of houses and properties. An English based would-be house purchaser may agree to buy a house, allow the seller to move all his property from the house and purchase another property and then, without any apparent reason at all, cancel the sale, leaving the vendor in an unpleasant predicament, to say the least.

Not so in Scotland, for once one has made an offer for a house in writing and that offer has been accepted there is, no going back, for the buyer has agreed to buy the property and under Scottish Legal Form such a transaction is a cast iron deal. Solicitors always warn would-be English buyers of this fact and, the type of person who dithers about, buying a property, cancelling the agreement at the last minute, to the distress of yet another would-be house seller, may investigate the possibility of buying a property in Scotland but the obligations of a Scottish contract usually dissuades him from proceeding further.

To cut my tale short, I travelled to East Mey in midwinter to view the property only to find the croft surrounded by marsh, although I could see little of the land because of the driving, blinding rain. I contented myself with the fact that this was exceptional weather by any standards and that the Heavens simply didn't hold enough water to allow two consecutive days of heavy rain. Thus I promptly bought the cottage together with another acre of land, which I was later to discover was made up of broken masonry with a liberal sprinkling of adders. Indeed, it was not until another year or so had passed that I was to discover that the day I had spent exploring the property was fairly clement by Caithnessian standards, and that while, for nine months of the year the weather in Caithness is bad – for the remaining three months, the weather is terrible!

CHAPTER 10

Coronary Times

A series of events came to a head on that fateful day in June 1985 and these events probably contributed to the massive coronary I sustained on that day but once again I fear I have run ahead of my tale.

On reflection my life had been an absolute muddle until that time and, despite the fact that I believed I was a more than competent teacher, my professional life was in chaos. I disliked my headmaster intensely and the feeling was reciprocated. Furthermore, the school was literally falling to pieces discipline-wise and the sight of distraught men and women facing a crowd of hostile children became all too common. It is a curious fact that, despite the notions of A. S. Neil and others of Summerhill persuasion, children like order and discipline. By discipline I don't mean the 'flog 'em and flog 'em again' tactics of my own childhood, for I had loathed and dreaded my own teachers. However, I do believe that both children and dogs enjoy an orderly atmosphere and as many of the classrooms in the school were little short of bedlam, few of the children enjoyed coming to school. Later during the year the Education Authority closed down the establishment that the newspapers referred to as 'the worst school in the Midlands', but truth be told, the school was a great deal worse than the papers described.

The staff had fallen to plotting coups to oust the head and, indeed, the head's wife had been ousted by her own staff, but such was the disunity of our staff that all attempts at a coup, a proper coup, fell apart before fruition and the school continued to stumble, bumble and tumble on. Perhaps the act of planning coups was all that kept the staff sane. Yet each day the place became more chaotic and it became inevitable that once the Education Authority started to reorganise, our school would be closed and its pupils and staff scattered to the wind.

I stayed well clear of coups and other petty bickerings which were taking place each and every day, for I had other interests. Each year I contrived to attempt what I loosely referred to as a 'project'. For instance, on the Christmas following my fortieth birthday two students and I constructed a raft out of plastic sewage pipes and sailed it down the River Severn from Shrewsbury to the Bristol Channel. The staff discussed my project, concluded I was NUTS and then went back to plotting against the headmaster.

However, in 1985 I had decided to break a team of German Shepherd Dogs to a sled, or rig, and run the dogs in harness and such thoughts were uppermost in my mind during the months that led up to my coronary. The staff, no doubt, heard my excited babblings, wrote me off as stark raving mad yet once again, and then went back to plotting yet another abortive coup against the head. Meanwhile, I began to punctuate my already very full social life with intensive reading sessions, designed to allow me to acquire knowledge about sleds and sled-dogs, and I confess I had much to learn.

My interest had been kindled by my father's library of Jack London books. My childhood, marred by my fearsome stammer, had been a lonely one and I spent much of my time with my head buried in one of London's tales of the frozen north. In these tales half-wild sled-dogs, more wolf than domesticated dog, hauled mail across frozen tundra, fought each other for leadership once the day's haul was over, dominant, primordial and furiously primitive. Thus, while other lads of my age fantasised of toppling the Japanese from the fortress of Iwo Jima or playing for Blackburn Rovers, my daydreams concerned blinding blizzards, whiteouts through which a man drove a team of prick-eared husky dogs, a spit away from pure-bred wolves. Yet it was to be a full forty years before I had the chance to explore the real world of sled-dogs and to realise that London's experience of the land beyond the snowline was both limited and inaccurate.

London simply enjoyed what I considered to be a rather unwholesome passion for wolves and all things lupine. He signed his letters to Sinclair Lewis, who furnished London with the plots for many books, 'Lone Wolf', and called his financially ruinous mansion 'The Wolf Shack'. To London, the wolf typified all that was beautiful, honourable and noble – and perhaps in many ways he was correct. Yet wolves were never the courageous beasts of Jack London legend and avoided direct conflict with man. The wolves of his tales would rather die than scavenge and turned their faces to the icy winds, sitting out the freezing winter with dignity. When the natives of Alaska and neighbouring Canadian Yukon found that the blood of southern dogs, setters, pointers, German Shepherd Dogs, Labradors had sullied the pure husky type sled-dogs, Jack London's Inuits and Indians allowed sled-dog bitches to be chained in the forests and tundra so that passing male wolves could mate with them and thus preserve the best qualities of the Arctic sled-dogs. London knew little of dogs and, frankly, could not have been more wrong.

In reality when the goldfields of Alaska and Yukon played out in the early 1900s – and it cost sixty million dollars to mine sixteen million dollars worth of gold, the mining camps became ghost towns where the odd, curious tourist found his ways during the brief, bright summer months. Southern dogs, the pointers, collies, German Shepherd Dogs and Labradors, so despised by the wolf-loving Jack London, mingled with the huskies bred by the local Indian and Eskimo peoples and produced the Alaskan husky, a type of dog which has proven vastly superior to the native Alaskan and Yukon sled-dogs. The new breed was stronger, faster and, despite London's misgivings, equally as hardy as native-bred dogs.

The fact is that, with encouragement, virtually any breed of medium or fairly large dog can be taught to pull a sled plus 200lb of freight. In the USA teams of brightly spotted Dalmatians, pointers, Irish setters and the curious Targhee hounds – a hybrid between the Irish setter and a staghound – have not only been taught to pull sleds but have competed in short races and have achieved great success against the traditional husky-type sled-dogs.

I was therefore quite aware that Polly, her daughters and granddaughters could be taught to pull a sled and set out to finding someone who had not only some skill but a training rig to which I could harness my team to encourage the dogs to pull. I feel the expression 'training rig' needs an explanation. A training rig usually consists of a modified three-wheeled tricycle fitted with a contraption to which a harness attachment could be welded. I hasten to add that I don't mean a child's tricycle but a larger adaptation of an old-fashioned man or woman's bicycle. Some rigs are quite simply trolley-type affairs which can be steered with one's feet. These are usually fairly dangerous contraptions as a sled dog team moves at a fair lick and it would require a man with the reflexes of a Chinese martial arts film actor to steer one.

Meanwhile, back at the ranch, once more my social life was in tatters. I have an amazing ability to make relationships with totally unsuitable women who then promptly set to divest me of what little property I seem to have acquired. Damn it, I've acquired such little wealth in my lifetime that it is a shame that various women have denuded all my worldly possessions. In 1985 I had somehow or other entered into a relationship with a totally unsuitable woman to whom I was never attracted and, on reflection, realise wasn't attracted to me. To cut a long story short, she borrowed my car and declined to return it. It was one of the only new cars I have ever been able to afford and after I had paid the very last instalment of my hire purchase agreement the good lady absconded with it and using slightly more legal terminology (via a solicitor) said, 'Okay sucker, come and get it if you can afford it. The damn car is mine now.' Well, I couldn't afford it, besides which I am an incredibly weak sort of person. Thus I found myself on foot once again, sans car and sans all the property which the good lady could carry away from my home – in my car I must add. If the expression 'There's one born every minute' is true, on my birth there must have been a twelve hour lapse, for I am the sucker of all suckers.

There is, I believe, a Texan proverb – 'A man on foot is no man at all' – and in the weeks following the departure of the good lady (with my car) I was to appreciate the truth of the statement. However, I had little time to consider my car-less state for I was hotfoot on the trail to Caithness with some builders who were to help repair my broken-down croft in Caithness. I bundled Polly onboard the lorry and for six hundred miles we travelled north amidst cement, sand and curious stony aggregate, the nature and use of which I have yet to discover.

It was June, a time when the latitude of Caithness ensures that darkness resides for only two or so hours a night. During the other twenty-two hours of daylight I worked – oh, how I worked – labouring for two bands of workmen, mixing quantities of cement similar to the amount used in the construction of the Great Pyramid. When I completed one load I had little time to pause and rest, for the other team began cursing me loudly for my failure to bring quantities of bricks. At night I fell into my sleeping bag and slept a dreamless sleep, to awake stiff and sore to face yet another agonising session of labouring. The work took on the nature of a torture designed by Olympian gods and goddesses and, truth to tell, I was too tired to join the team in the 10pm trip to the local pub. I ate standing and ate all the wrong food, so my hiatus hernia began to play up, making the agony of the day tenfold. Two long, painful weeks later with the work only half completed I drove the gangs home – a seventeen hour trip from Caithness to Lichfield – only to be greeted by an artist girlfriend with whom I spent the following night.

No one, not even the fittest sexual, athlete could take this pace of life, and I was scarcely the fittest of people. So it was at 9am on the morning of June 5th, 1985 I experienced the most agonising pain to my solar plexus. Bicarbonate of soda, my cure-all for all the illnesses the sun sucks up, failed to ease the agony and by 10am I realised that I was experiencing something a great deal more serious than the irritation of my hiatus hernia. The agony continued to increase and in the ambulance taking me to Lichfield I realised I was experiencing what is known in medical parlance as a myocardial infarction, or in layman's terms, a heart attack.

CHAPTER 11

A Time To Reflect

I believe it was the German philosopher Nietzsche who said 'That which does not kill me makes me stronger', from which I realise that Nietzsche had never experienced a heart attack. To date at least, nothing in my life has been more debilitating. I stayed in intensive care for two weeks only to be warned each day by a caring doctor to change my lifestyle or to suffer dire consequences. I was forty seven years old living a lifestyle which would have exhausted a bumble bee and my body had decided to rebel at the way I was treating it. My coronary, my myocardial infraction, my plain honest to goodness heart attack, was a warning that a total eclipse was on the way if I didn't change my way of life.

On the fourth day after my heart attack, against all advice I uncoupled my medical attachments and attempted a trip to the ward toilet some twelve yards away. It was only then that I realised just how debilitating the heart attack had been. I swayed drunkenly as I attempted my first step and only after three or four attempts did I manage to reach the toilet. Never have I felt more exhausted and finally, I realised just how close a brush with death I had experienced. Once back in bed, scolded by the nurses and fellow patients, I sank into the deep sleep I had experienced after the one and only charity marathon I attempted to run.

Friends visited me a shade too regularly to make life comfortable, unaware that I felt like a boxer who put up a shameful performance in the ring the previous night and needed to be left alone to recover from both injury and loss of pride. Mandy and Steve, two dear and much loved associates, kept me informed about my kennels. Fathom, my elderly in-whelp lurcher bitch, had gone feral, refusing to be caught, living off the wild and scavenging and finally producing her litter in a hole in the hedgerow in Barlow's field. My truly great lurcher bitch Merab had been born in this hole, for Fathom delighted in a feral existence.

My terriers were distributed to friends, alas never to be brought back once their new owners bonded with them, although crusty old aggressive Vampire stayed in kennels, unwanted by friends because of his ferocious disposition.

Polly remained indoors, to be let out once a day by Mandy Bennett. Not once did Polly foul in the house or destroy a single item of furniture despite the fact she saw few people during my two week stay in hospital. Usually a dog confined in such a manner develops a disorder known as separation anxiety and begins to display peculiar habits. Often dogs subjected to such isolation, day in day out isolation, will start destroying items of clothes and furniture associated with the absent owner. Some will pull down items of clothing and either lie on them or carry them to the sleeping box. Others will behave in a rather more unsavoury manner and after seeking out items of the owner's clothing, foul on them. Separation from an owner, particularly an owner who has paid much attention to a dog induces all manner of peculiar behaviour patterns. Not so with Polly, for Polly behaved impeccably in my absence and on my return greeted me gently, displaying none of the wild exuberance most dogs would when a much loved owner returned after an absence. It was in fact as if she was actually aware of my frailty when I left the hospital.

Curiously I was more concerned about Polly's welfare than about Fathom's. Fathom was the most independent lurcher I have ever owned and had a sort of canine street knowledge that is hard to imagine. She was certainly capable of keeping herself in an area where game birds and small animals abounded, and frequently went native. She was a natural thief, a fearsome opportunist and the complete omnivore. She ate voraciously everything and anything and if times were hard and she failed to kill or find that day, she would travel several miles to beg food from Pete Beddows who lived on the other side of the A38. Yet she was such a wonderful hunter that she seldom used begging to fill her stomach. I have owned many lurchers and seen a great deal many more but I have yet to see a dog who was more adept at stalking her quarry. She would see a rabbit, or a fairly large bird, and then crawl belly down in the manner of a farm cat until she was within range of her quarry and then make one lightening lunge to secure her prey. Indeed I was not the slightest bit worried that Fathom would survive without help from others. Yet when I returned, I whistled to her and she crawled out of the hole she had dug to whelp her puppies and greeted me cordially, as if I had never been away. Steve had repeatedly tried to catch her or lure her into one of the kennels but with a wag of the tail she had managed to stay out of reach. Yet, on my return, she greeted me as if nothing had been amiss.

I had ample time to reflect on the aimless nature of my life as I lay in the intensive care ward surrounded by those less fortunate than I. For the first time in my life I had a chance to break from the teaching profession. Few teachers survive a coronary to return to teaching the wildly disruptive children like those that had been in my care, and live to tell the tale. Any ailment that leaves the recipient below par renders the teacher vulnerable to all the problems a probationary teacher experiences in his or her first traumatic year of teaching. Yet I lacked the courage to cut the tether that bound me to a job I hated and as I lay abed recovering from my heart attack, I resigned myself to returning to the school when I had recovered.

So it was, after two weeks intensive care, I returned home to Polly and Co., tired, exhausted, listless and weak as a kitten. During my spell in hospital I had resolved to change my way of life, to eat sensibly, avoiding the lightening fast food which had been my staple diet for the late twenty or so years, to go to bed at a reasonable hour and to avoid contact with any women who would be likely to cause me stress. However, like poor, sad Oscar Wilde I can resist anything but temptation and as soon as I was able to walk I plunged back into the same chaotic lifestyle I had promised to avoid.

Within a month of my release I became involved with a young, very beautiful and totally unsuitable mature student who was reading a BA in English at Birmingham University and in next to no time I was back in the same destructive social whirl I sought to avoid. My six months at home recovering from my heart attack I wasted, and squandered perhaps, but during that time I came to know Polly really well and to fully appreciate her great worth and truly amazing versatility.

Fathom led me to her litter of puppies in a dug out rabbit earth in Gerald Barlow's field some two days after I arrived home, and I tottered after her to view the puppies. They had been sired by her grandson Ilan and the incestuous brood were as alike as peas in a pod. I was too weak and shaky to carry them back to kennels and I therefore left them for a few days to allow Eddie to recover them. The first week or so of a puppy's life is relatively unimportant in relation to it's future development, providing the whelp is warm and well fed, and the whelp lives in what Dunbar calls a 'sensory void'. Hence I walked the twenty-five yards to the hedgerow lair each day with Polly in attendance only to check on the well-being of the whelps.

Polly would stand, head held to one side to listen to the squeaks and squeals which emanated from the dug out and enlarged rabbit burrow, and as expected came into milk in a matter of days. She was the essential Earth Mother figure, the sort of animal that adopted virtually any orphan regardless of species. Thus it was when Eddie finally dug out the litter of whelps whose eyes had only just opened, Polly adopted them without question. It was fortunate perhaps for Fathom, now restricted by the kennel in which I had incarcerated her, decided to abandon her puppies. She was never a great mother and preferred to hunt rather than suckle puppies. It was therefore left to Polly to rear the litter.

A bland but pleasant summer slipped and slithered into a cold and wet autumn during which time I became even more aware of Polly's versatility. As the season progressed I fetched out my rabbiting nets and went ferreting with Fathom and Polly in attendance. Fathom, for all her free spirit attitude, was an excellent ferreter's dog and for those not au fait with the arcane world of ferreting I shall explain what a ferreter's dog is required to do.

A ferreter's dog is required to find an inhabited burrow and mark the presence of a rabbit in the burrow. Rabbits dig many burrows but decide to live in only one set of holes. A ferreter will place nets over any hole which is likely to house a rabbit but, without a dog to mark the presence of a rabbit, he might spend an entire day fruitlessly netting-up uninhabited burrows. A properly trained ferreting dog will ignore empty burrows and start to point or scratch at an inhabited lair, literally telling the ferreter that these are the set of holes which are worth netting.

Fathom's family had been great ferreter's dogs and her daughter, Merab, the best I have ever seen but Polly, while she had chased and caught dozens of rabbits had never marked one to ground. Yet once she observed Fathom marking a burrow and realised that a ferret inserted in the burrow usually induced a rabbit to bolt, she seemed to understand, and I found her marking inhabited burrows, touching the mouth of the earth to indicate the presence of a rabbit, and finally standing back to await the placing of rabbit nets and the insertion of a ferret. She snatched at the first rabbit she saw entangled in a net but once chided for her misdeed she seemed to understand and simply stood back and although quivering with excitement, refrained from grabbing the netted rabbits.

First time dog owners and 'dog writers' alike might be forgiven for that essential scientific sin anthropomorphism (crediting animals with human qualities such as honour, guilt, superior perspicacity etc.) once they have owned a dog such as Polly. Polly seemed to understand virtually everything I said to her. If I devised a task, sometimes even a meaningless childish type of task, and showed I was pleased with any attempt she made to perform that task, she became ecstatic with delight and learned at an amazing rate. Once while ferreting, and I admit I am remiss about picking up all the nets I have set, I realised I was two nets short. I was perhaps four hundred yards from the burrow and exhausted, as only those recovering from a major illness can be, so in as much hope as despair I said to Polly, 'Go back and fetch the nets.' I had from time to time sent her back to fetch a glove or ball I had deliberately dropped but she could not possibly have understood what a 'net' was. Yet she returned to the spot we were ferreting, casting all the way to detect some object which carried my scent. On arriving at the burrow, a spot which must have reeked of the pungent scent of ferret and rabbit, she found one of the pegged-down nets, lifted it and carried it gently to hand. I praised her gently for effusive praise disturbed her somewhat, and sent her back for the other net which she found and carried to hand. Teaching her was indeed a pleasure.

On the subject of a dog's remarkable scenting ability, a tale will suffice to explain her remarkable powers. My one and only claim to fame is that I conducted what is now universally accepted as being one of the worst television interviews on record. As explained earlier I was interviewed by Richard Whitely who was bitten by one of my ferrets, which hung on like a bulldog indulging in a game rather that perpetrating an act of savagery, this interview was my small claim to fame but one which brought me a host of television interviews and media attention.

One television team on hearing I had purchased a 3½ acre patch of scrub and bog, euphemistically referred to as a croft, in Caithness and that I travelled there each school holiday in order to keep my sanity and to prepare myself for what television producers called, a spot of 'going native', sent a camera team to Caithness one holiday to film the lifestyle of an eccentric. Such was the way television producers regarded me. I suppose.

The television team arrived without warning and were delighted to find that my croft was devoid of furnishings and that I cooked my food on an open fire. How wonderfully effete the team were, a star's flight from myself, so different in fact as to appear to be members of another species. They regarded hardship as having to stay at a four star hotel and not to be able to drink fine wine, (one of the team sent south for a particular vintage wine, costing £45). I was earning £105 a week at the time and my palate was ill-used to the bitter, astringent wine he gave me to sample. For two weeks the team followed me, probably laughing up their sleeves at my simple way of life and the fact I fished in the bay using a 100 yard gill net to catch pollack which was cooked over a fire of peat I had cut and dried the summer previous. They watched with a look akin to boredom on their faces as I snared rabbits to feed myself and my dogs, Polly, Fathom and the ageing lurcher bitch Penguin, the mother of Fathom. Yet amazingly a curious event triggered their interest in a manner that was difficult to appreciate.

I sat on the pebble beds at Harrow Harbour near the Castle of Mey, one of the homes of the Queen Mother and idly cast a pebble onto a pebble bank comprising a hundred thousand or so identical pebbles. Polly, who observed my idle gesture, walked to the spot where the pebble had fallen and fetched it to hand. A look of near amazement suffused the bored face of the camera man, who was obviously tiring of his tour of rustic life and he asked me to repeat the performance. Polly instantly entered into the spirit of the game and fetched the pebble to hand. The film crew became ecstatic and put small marks upon pebbles asking me to throw them amongst identical pebbles and requesting Polly retrieve them, which she did with contemptuous ease, for she was probably as mystified about the crews' enthusiasm as I was.

How little the average man knows about dogdom and the behaviour of their pets! A dog's olfactory senses are many times as keen as those of a man and hence Polly experienced little difficulty retrieving any pebble I had handled for humans are heavily scented creatures who leave the taint of their presence wherever they go. Indeed, so unpleasant is the scent of man, even heavily deodorised man, that Laverack, a behaviourist, believes that when, semi-upright man, more simian than hominid, left the trees the trees to make the first faltering steps in the hostile savannah, one of the qualities which helped save him from an early extinction was his unpleasant smell, for few predators find the flesh of man attractive.

Yet the misplaced enthusiasm of the television team at Polly's ability to retrieve a pebble from a pebble-strewn beach did much to confirm my beliefs about myself and my relationship with my fellow teachers. I had hitherto believed that my inability to mingle with anyone in the same profession, my rejection by fellow teachers, was simply due to my gaucherie, for I was too aware of my social awkwardness when I met those who spoke quiet, confident 'didactic', rather than simple English. Now I began to realise that my rejection was due to the fact that I was quite simply an atavism, a throwback perhaps, a creature out of place in time. Not only was I not ready for the next millennium I was socially incapable of dealing with people who represented the present. I have been lonely many times in my life but most lonely in the midst of a

crowd. Yet I have always had an almost amazing affinity with animals and almost instinctively understood the ways of birds and beasts. Some years ago I had confided in Moses Aaron Smith, the settled Romany friend of mine, that I was able to detect the presence of an in-season bitch by scent. Mo raised one of his bushy eyebrows and cut me down with one of his glib epigrams, 'S'pose its alright,' he uttered but added, 'providing yer don't get excited by the smell.' On a more serious note he added, 'I wouldn't tell too many people about that although, Bri' as he always said when he was feeling rather sorry for me.

The spring holiday was the last time I would regard Caithness as a holiday home, however, for long before the Easter holiday was upon me, I realised that I must leave the teaching profession forever and transfer my 'goods and flocks' to Caithness.

For the first time in my life I felt I was unable to keep order in chaos. Ordinarily I entered the room, quietened the class and shut the door on the sheer bedlam that prevailed in the rest of the school. Now I found difficult children answering back, refusing to be browbeaten into submission. One of my many Godchildren became very difficult in class one day in April 1986 and I knew that I must leave the school. My coronary had weakened not only my body, leaving me breathless and exhausted after a contretemps with a child but had weakened my self resolve.

So it was that I submitted my resignation to an all too grateful headmaster, sold my house by auction for less than it was worth and, like a latter day Abraham, travelled to Caithness taking with me my predatory menagerie. So it now behoves me to explain what I mean by 'my predatory menagerie'.

CHAPTER 12

Polly and the Predatory Menagerie

I'm afraid this chapter is a bit like a large slice of the biblical book of *Genesis* – Abraham begat Isaac who begat Jacob who begat ... but I'm afraid anyone who seriously attempts to produce a kennel of working dogs will need to be able to write such a genealogical account. Incidentally, before proceeding further, I think it wise to discuss the real meaning of the word pedigree, which is incorrectly used by the majority of dog breeders. Pedigree, is derived from the French *pied de grue*, foot of the crane (three toes to the rear, one toe to the front which was the symbol used by primitive genealogists to illustrate descent from ancestors).

I seldom went anywhere without my lurchers Fathom and her daughter Merab, for to anyone leading the life I led and intended to lead, such dogs are priceless. Those who are not au fait with the subject of lurchers, and few conventional dog keepers are, lurchers are crossbred dogs derived from greyhounds mated to dogs of 'base-blood' – collies, Bedlington terriers etc. It must be bewildering to anyone involved with the breeding of Kennel Club registered pure-bred dogs that anyone would seek to cross or bastardise a greyhound (the most blue blooded of dogs) with another breed, but greyhounds whilst being the fastest of dogs are scarcely the most intelligent and tractable of canines. Furthermore, they have somewhat limited olfactory senses, although some will hunt nose down in the manner of a beagle. Collies are tractable and for some reason, which I confess in unknown to me, have a strong sense of smell. Thus a combination of greyhound and collie blood confers on the hybrid what Dan Russell once described as 'the body of a greyhound and the wisdom of Solomon.'

As a scientist I am not given to anthropomorphic thinking and I am most reluctant to credit animals with human qualities ('My dog is like one of the family.' – Question – 'Which one?') but there have been occasions when I have watched Fathom and Merab perform actions which must have been motivated by some sense akin to thought. When she has sighted 'catchable' game far out in the middle of a field Fathom had controlled her desire to attempt to chase it and hence lose the 'catch' but instead had crawled belly down, using every bush, every obstacle, every area of cover to stalk her prey and quite often succeeded in catching by dint of this ploy. Her nose was breathtaking as was her mother Penguin's and her grandfather Hein's, and she could canter down a forestry or woodland ride stopping in mid flight to point a bird or a rabbit. She was an excellent catch dog by any standards but old long before I began my stay in Caithness. I find it almost impossible not to write about her as if she was still alive for together with Polly she occupied such a big part of my life. During my sixth year in Caithness she became very thin and listless and, unwisely perhaps, I dosed her with an anthelmintic, a worming medicine called Dichlorophen, in order to rid her of tapeworms. My action precipitated her death, or so I believe as she sickened rapidly and died some three weeks later. She died during an icy spell and I waited three weeks for the ground to thaw in order that I might bury her. She was twenty seven years old and her catches and company had helped me through some of the desperate years during my spell in the teaching profession.

Yet if truth be told, her daughter Merab, wrought by mating Fathom to her grandson, was a hundred times better. It is perhaps time to explain my incestuous breeding schemes.

During that spell of my life when I gambled so frequently that I considered it more sensible to pay my teacher's salary directly to the Hall Green Greyhound Stadium's tote, I acquired many of the superstitious practices which are associated with gambling. One of these practices dictated that should a card player who was experiencing success at the gaming table leave the room for some reason and on returning find someone sitting in his place, the game concluded at that point for 'with the seat went the luck'.

It is a policy I have always adopted when breeding dogs. I'll explain. If I found that a particular dog of any breed had many desirable qualities as a hunter, guard or work dog, I then perpetuated the family either by inbreeding, mating the animal to a very close relative, brother, sister, father, mother etc. or by a less intense method of incestuous matings known as line breeding, continuing the line by mating more distantly related animals, cousins, grandparents, grandchildren, aunts, uncles. There is a notion that such consanguinity produces inferior animals and deformities found only in the pages of an H. P. Lovecraft, novel and to a certain extent such thinking is justified, for inbreeding certainly brings all the undesirable recessives to the surface. Conversely such a breeding programme enhances the virtues found in a strain. So it was with Merab and her equally inbred granddaughter Phaedra:

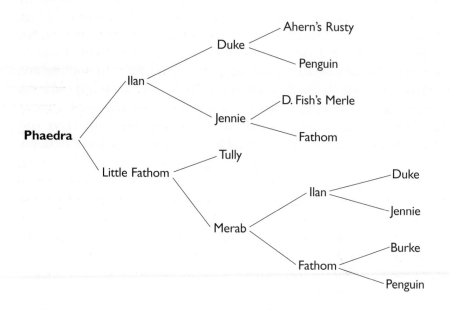

In addition to my lurchers, I brought my small kennel of working bearded collies, all of which were descended from my bitch Muirhead's Dot, with me on my trek north. For those who have only seen bearded collies at Kennel Club shows might I mention that the working bearded collie, the sort still worked by occasional shepherds in the Highlands and Southern Uplands, is a very different animal from the show bred bearded collie. Less hirsute, possessing a shadow of the flowing coat of the show bred animal, the working bearded collie has the intelligence of its more glabrous relative, the working Border Collie, the standard equipment, so to speak, of the British shepherd. A tale will suffice to illustrate this point.

I purchased Dot as a grown dog (not a good practice as adult beardies change hands reluctantly and are frequently unwilling to settle with new owners) from an advert in the Scottish Farmer and travelled up to the Borders to collect her.

On her journey back to Lichfield she displayed a great fear of me, a terror I have come to expect when grown bearded collies arrive in an alien environment, and hence I brought her into the house to allow me to become accustomed to her and her to me. She flashed into my bedroom as soon as I attempted to stroke her, however, and to my horror I heard the click of the crossbar catch as she hurled herself against the window. I raced to the bedroom to find Dot's derriere in the room but her head and forepaws outside the bedroom. Too late I watched her scrabble through the window and vanish into the night.

I believe I searched for her for two days in the blinding icy rain but found not a trace of her. I advertised her loss in Lichfield and in Whittington Post Office but while a dozen or so people telephoned to commiserate or to lure me into following spurious leads, Dot was nowhere to be seen and I cursed the fact I had paid a full month's salary to purchase a trained sheepdog and the fact that the crossbar catches on my windows were ill-fitting and easily sprung. However, I was later to rejoice at my inability to fit windows in my badly built little cottage, but once again I run ahead of my tale.

One evening I was visited by a woman who was enjoying, or perhaps suffering, one of those short-lived relationships with me, for all my lady friends seemed as glad to say 'Goodbye' as I am to see them go. Amaliea was what Moses had referred to rather unkindly as 'a failed opera singer', I was a 'failed' teacher, Ray was a 'failed' joiner, and Amiliea's one claim to fame was a short spell as an understudy soprano at La Scala Milan. After that her life had been one hurry on down descent until she reached rock bottom and teamed up with the failed school teacher!

On the evening in question I was rather at a loss, translating a book of spells sent me by a lunatic who was seeking eternal life – a curse rather than a blessing I thought at the time – as I tried to make sense of the hocus pocus in the pages of the mad man's precious grimoire. Amaliea arrived in a sulky mood, for despite her rather gorgeous Latin looks she had failed an audition for a part in *Carmen*, and criticised my method of picking up 'pin money', an unfortunate choice of expression considering the nature of the document I was trying to translate! 'Don't you get scared bothering with this sort of lunatic?' she spat out spitefully, referring to the Macintosh-clad man who had brought the document for translation – a gaunt sallow skinned man who belonged amongst a Dennis Wheatley fan club meeting, I thought at the time. Quite suddenly Polly pricked up her ears and growled softly at something I couldn't discern. 'Even the dog is alerted to the fact you've invited something evil home' she spluttered, pointing at the badly worn grimoire on the kitchen table. My opera singer honestly believed in the Gothic horror notion that evil must be invited into one's home. Amaliea continued in a voice which indicated the contempt she was feeling for me and told a tale of a production of Verdi's *Aïda* which became accursed when one of the cast developed a somewhat more than casual interest in diabolism. Polly however was standing at the kitchen door, ears erect but wagging her tail as if pleased by the sounds to which she was listening.

I stood and opened the kitchen door allowing Polly to run the passage way to my bedroom where she stood wagging her tail in delight and so without further ado I opened the bedroom door, flicking on the light via the ill-fitting switch I had promised to repair. To my amazement I caught sight of Dot's rump disappearing via the top window.

I was more amazed than startled by the sight and reflected on the perspicacity of any dog which could not only escape via a top light (despite the ill-fitting catch) but could return at will to the spot from whence she had escaped. What was more amazing was the fact that for six weeks she had managed to survive undetected in a district which scarcely presented an non-hunting collie bitch with a plenitude of food. However, the next night I approached my bedroom from Gerald Barlow's field, sealed the window and trapped Dot within the house – 'Thereby demonstrating you are more intelligent that a bloody collie,' Moses had sneered when I related the tale.

Dot was found to be not the slightest bit harmed by her six weeks of exposure at the coldest time of the year. Somehow she must have found some way of feeding herself, possibly by rummaging in the dustbins of the nearby village, perhaps eating road casualty birds and rabbits, for beardies are seldom fleet enough to catch rabbits on a regular basis. I also suspect she had led a nocturnal existence, perhaps sleeping in my bedroom by day and vanishing like 'the fabric of a vision faded' whenever she heard my car arrive at 4pm. Whatever lifestyle she had led she was in excellent health and in three weeks she was in season again. I mated her to the famous Turnbull's Blue and produced Shergar and Cher, the foundation stock of the modern Working Bearded Collie Association, the logo of which is a head study of Cher. Inbreeding to Dot produced not only truly excellent workers but, alas, two animals which manifested cerebellum degeneration, the result of an autosomal recessive gene found in some bearded collies but that, as Kipling would say ' is another tale', one left to another time perhaps.

Poor Dot, and why do all my tales have a sad ending? She died just three weeks ago after a terrier attacked her. Veterinary treatment proved to be of no avail and she slipped and slithered into death over a period of twelve days. Her life had been a long one and her progeny many, for she was twenty four years old when I buried her next to Ilan the father of Merab and an old friend with whom Dot was once kennelled. Owning her made me acutely aware of Mark Twain's ability to spin an aphorism, for it is indeed a sad thing that a dog's life is so much shorter than that of its owner.

Meanwhile Polly had been mated to her grandfather Asoka Zorbay, a yellow, gaunt and ugly dog but one who produced splendid litters of puppies. It appears that like does not always breed like for his daughters Felicity and Bimbo were truly beautiful white bitches and, unlike the modern German Shepherd Dogs, strong and powerfully built. I believe that the modern German Shepherd Dog is far too lightly built and that the bitches need to be a great deal stronger if they are to have the deterrent value a guard dog should have.

One of Polly's puppies was sold as a drug detection dog; I believe this male inherited some of the acute scenting qualities Polly possessed. I must admit that I had some trepidation about selling a dog which was to be used for drug detection, for at that time I tended to believe the old wives' tale concerning the lives of such animals. There were tales of drug addicted dogs furiously searching luggage for illicit substances and finally collapsing in limp heaps if the substance could not be detected. Nothing could be further from the truth as explained earlier. Unfortunately one of the German Shepherd Dogs I sold as a detection dog activated a tumbler device in its joyful search for its beloved 'toy' with terrifying consequences, I must add. I must also add that I no longer sell puppies to people who intend to use these dogs as explosives seekers.

Polly had bred a second litter, this one fathered by a different sire. Zorbay had died quite suddenly but then he was a great age when he sired Bimbo and Felicity. I settled for a dog known as Kabyune Quota, a fine very white male bred from a coloured sire and dam. Quota carried bloodlines to Bandit Von Leiberg but was sired by a German import, Lex Von Steintahl.

What a difference a change of sire wrought! Polly produced four puppies – she was never a big breeder – and while three were very white one was dingy cream colour. Genetically they were perhaps more sound than those produced by Zorbay, for Zorbay carried lines to dogs which were known as 'fitters' (epileptics) and animals which were known to produce dysplastic dogs. Quota carried none of these lines yet the litter sired by him were in many ways less pleasing.

Fashions change in the dog world almost as frequently as in the rag trade. Polly's line were big heavy-boned animals, Polly herself weighed nearly 100 lbs. at five years of age, and with this great bulk went a quiet, phlegmatic disposition. This type had once been popular amongst German Shepherd Dog breeders and many of the early coloured champions were incredibly strong, big boned animals. However recent German imports were very different. A faster, lighter type of animal was now becoming popular in Germany and with this new shape went a more restless, hyperactive disposition. A criticism of this new type was that they were difficult to live with, not a grammatically correct statement but I know all to well what the breeders meant.

I kept back two bitches from the union, a very white bitch I called Beltane and the decidedly yellow bitch which I named Pagan. Beltane had Polly's gentle disposition, Pagan did not. She was a restless lightly built animal, little more than 45 lbs when fully grown and only 22½ inches at the shoulder. In kennels she caused Hell by her restless pacing and her incessant barking which could be triggered by the most trivial of events, a leaf rustling outside her kennels, a branch tapping against the window of the house, virtually anything could trigger a cacophony of hysterical barking which abated only when Pagan became exhausted. In fact, before I left Lichfield she became a victim of one of the most terrible kennel fights I have ever seen, although I confess I was partly to blame for the battle, cue for a spot of canine psychology and a switch of species I'm afraid.

In 1951 the behaviourist Steiniger conducted a series of interesting experiments which would be condemned as illegal if conducted today. Steiniger gathered together a group of wild rats obtained from different wild colonies and incarcerated them in an escape-proof pen some 30 square yards in area. For a while the rats wandered about snapping at each other but if two rats collided on a run, displaying little real antipathy to one another. That is until a male and female rat paired up! Whereupon the female of the pair sought out and slew every other doe rat and the male attacked and killed every buck.

The pair then promptly settled down to an idyllic existence and produced ratlings which mated incestuously producing grandchildren for the original pair. Rats are a little like humans in some ways, a little more honourable perhaps, but like their human counterparts, rat grandparents are very indulgent where grandchildren are concerned and the original pair allowed their grandchildren all manner of liberties. Truly Steiniger's rat compound must have seemed like a Garden of Eden to its rodent occupants.

Then one day Steiniger introduced a strange rat from another wild colony. At first the other rats ignored it until they discovered the strange rat had a different smell. They tore the hapless brute to pieces and then, to Steiniger's surprise, the whole colony started fighting to the death – once indulgent grandparents attacked and killed hitherto much adored ratling grandchildren and brother fought brother, sister slaying sister until once more only a single pair of rats remained. Curiously a similar experiment was conducted with house mice with identical results.

It appears that social animals enjoy a structured lifestyle, a lifestyle where each and every member of the group knows its place and behaves to its superiors and inferiors accordingly. A newcomer disrupts the pattern and causes fierce and bloody chaos, for a while at least.

Thus a kennel owner who keeps a family of dogs or a quiet content kennel of unrelated but structured dogs and bitches would do well not to bring a strange dog onto the premises, or at least not a mature strange dog or bitch. It is in fact sheer madness to allow a stranger to bring along his or her dog, and to allow them to see the kennel occupants through the kennel wires. Frenzied kennel fights often result from such actions and these kennel fights continue long after the strange dog has returned home. Huntsmen whose lives are intertwined with beagles, harriers, foxhounds and staghounds are especially careful about introducing new 'draught' hounds into kennels, particularly as such hounds are frequently draughted because their presence has disrupted their previous kennels. Such hounds are introduced gradually and the initial introductions are best conducted in the hunting field far away from the kennels, so that the strange hound acquires some of the scent of its new kennel mates before returning home. The pack must then be watched for several weeks after the introduction lest furious and lethal kennel fights should begin.

I make no excuse for what is to follow, for I knew full well Steiniger's findings and thought I understood them. Furthermore, for most of my life I have worked with animals living in a pack situation and was only too aware that flash fights are all too easily triggered by a new introduction to the kennels. My only defence is that I have always been putty in the hands of any attractive woman and here beginneth the tale proper!

Polly's second litter were fifteen months at the time I was approached by a thirty-year-old Whittington woman who asked me to board her dog while she went on holiday at some fashionable resort in Greece. Now the good lady was obviously seeking cheap boarding accommodation, for the animal for she knew full well that I had no boarding licence and could only accept her pet if I charged her nothing for its keep. Come to think of it, I must experience periods in my life when I become stark, staring undeniably mad for I even related to the good lady that a newcomer to the kennels could and most certainly would trigger the most savage of kennel fights but minutes later I was waving the lady goodbye and holding on to the leash of a very mongrelised bitch called Millie. Hell began to break loose forthwith.

Moses arrived shortly after the lady left and sneered at my stupidity. 'Why on earth have you taken on this creature,' he said pointing disparagingly with his foot at the ugly mongrel Millie who possessed all the unsightly features of the many breeds in her make-up. 'Daft you are,' he continued and added, 'They don't boil turnips softer than you are, mate,' before departing with a five gallon can of bitumen he had left at the kennels a week previous. Moses was, of course, correct.

I attempted to introduce Millie to the denizens of the kennels gradually, allowing my own dogs to watch and sniff her while she remained in the security of her kennel and only after a week of incarceration did I allow her to walk abroad amongst the pack. At first they swarmed around, the super-excitable Pagan and Beltane attempting to ride her not because of any lesbian interests but simply to demonstrate their superiority. When at last I deemed the pack had lost interest in Millie I set off down the lane, Millie running free and the rest of my dogs seemingly unconcerned by her presence – at least that is what I thought. However, on returning to my kennels the pack suddenly set about Millie in the gateway, although I still have to discover what insignificant action stimulated the attack.

It is extremely difficult to separate battling terriers, particularly when these fourteen pound grapplers are excited by the battle. It is doubly difficult to beat off some twelve or so medium and large sized dogs which are frantically trying to slay what they regard as an intruder in the kennels. However, I finally succeeded in locating the muddy and bloody Millie under the melee and, with a superhuman effort, hurled her over the fence into Barlow's field – a place which has acted as a sanctuary for many dogs which were in the process of being injured or killed in kennel fights. Millie did not hang around to witness what was happening in the run and promptly hightailed it to the house in Whittington, some mile and a half distant.

I fell against the fence exhausted by the Herculean task of hurling a fifty pound dog over a seven feet fence and felt a certain unhealthy tightness in my chest, but I had little chance to regain my composure and breath, for the pack, denied their victim, raged and finally set about Pagan who had been a participant in the battle. Once more I waded into the affray, receiving some terrible bites for my trouble and finally succeeded in kennelling the now injured Pagan and settling the others with a furious display of shouting, screaming and waving my arms in order to demonstrate my superiority. Breathless and, frankly, not a little frightened I gazed around the run at the slavering culprits, now wide-eyed with a mixture of fear and excitement. Even Polly, the most biddable of dogs, the most phlegmatic of creatures, had reverted to become a slavering fiend, eager to seek out and destroy her terrified daughter.

Lorenz refers to this somewhat odd behaviour pattern as intra-specific inter-family aggression but how like dogs humans can be. At the end of my first college year I witnessed a Hell raising night performed by students who had just completed their final examinations and were 'letting off steam' after a particularly taxing and traumatic term. The ritual behaviour patterns consisted of attacking the least popular student in the year and making his life a misery by dint of what can only be called, physical torture. The unpopular student in question had wisely absented himself that evening and so a band of supposedly cultured and intellectual young men, inflamed by drink perhaps, searched the campus to seek out their substitute victim. On failing to find him they chanced upon an innocuous and inoffensive student not noteworthy in any way and set about him with an unwholesome fury, breaking his arm and bruising him badly. Indeed, Kipling knew quite a lot about human behaviour when he wrote that one has only to scratch the veneer of civilised men to lay bare the most furious of savages. I watched the assault on the young man, whose only crime had been carrying a bundle of books which he was trying to sell, and made a mental note not to be present on the Hell raising night of my final year. Like poor bewildered Pagan, I was cursed with peculiarities which made me a victim of provocative victim syndrome, for no matter in which social group I find myself it is only a matter of time before I am adopting the role of the social outcast, the pariah, the Ishmael figure against whom every hand seems to be turned.

After the battle it was never safe to leave Pagan alone in the run in the company of other dogs. If I was present, the pack milled around in an aimless fashion apparently ignoring poor Pagan, but once I stepped out of the gate they began paying unwholesome attention to her. They would circle her, tails held high as if to intimidate or to provoke some reaction from her and should she snap at them they would rush her and attempt to kill the poor wretch. She was forced into enduring this torture for four long years before I took pity on her and gave the bitch to a lady in Dornoch. I saw her just before my departure from Caithness, an elderly, grey-faced, but still hyperactive bitch, of a type and disposition I have sought to breed out of the strain.

In a wild pack, bitches such as Pagan lead a miserable life and dwell on the outskirts of canine society. They are last to feed on a kill and seldom produce puppies, for breeding is the prerogative of the Alpha bitches of a pack. However, it is seldom that these animals are slain as a result of a pack battle of the sort so beloved by Jack London who knew little of dogs and canine behaviour. Pack fights, serious battles rather than petty squabbles are rare amongst wild dogs simply because they ensure a pack becomes inefficient in the hunt for food. A wretched bitch or dog downed by the rest of the pack will inflict savage bites during its death struggle, thereby rendering the pack unable to give of its best during a hunt for game. Outcast animals, social pariahs, are simply ostracised and ignored by the pack or driven out, finding difficulty in obtaining food or a safe den to sleep. Enough however of the peculiarities of Pagan, for I have described the last of my predatory menagerie.

However the logistics of moving such a group of animals from the Midlands to Caithness was complex, to say the least, and far beyond my limited mental capabilities. My dogs, particularly my lurchers, had once more attracted the attentions of thieves and the whole process of moving had to be conducted in a clandestine manner lest my absence provoked thieves into burgling my house for what little worldly possessions I still had. So it was that I moved to Caithness in a hired 30 cwt van, hired and driven by Steve, while I spent the seventeen hour trip amongst the dogs in the rear of the van, sandwiched between sacks of smelly offal and drenched by droplets of equally smelly condensation, resulting from the moisture from the dogs' breath meeting the cold roof of the van.

I had previously considered that I had recovered from my coronary and was once more fit and well. The trip convinced me otherwise and long before we left Perth – the halfway point of the trip, for cartographers are decidedly out of touch with the geography of Scotland – I felt decidedly ill. Dull pains wracked my chest and I felt the all too familiar ache down my left upper arm, clear indication that all was not well.

As it was I arrived drenched by the condensation, stinking of cows' tripes and exhausted beyond belief but I was left with the task of bedding down my team of dogs and feeding the pack before bathing and falling into a deep, dreamless sleep which lasted until noon the next day.

However, I had little chance to recover my long lost vitality or to recuperate from my coronary, for next day at 12.30pm my telephone rang and I was invited to conclude the film I was making for Yorkshire Television – cue for next chapter.

CHAPTER 13

A Somewhat Run Down Celebrity

I suppose the only criticism I can levy at television in general is that the majority of programmes give a totally false impression of people and places. For instance, anyone watching the programme *Taggart* might be forgiven for thinking that Glasgow is one huge unhallowed graveyard criss-crossed with motorways. Likewise anyone tuning into *Inspector Morse* or reading the books of Colin Dexter for that matter, might well imagine that a trip through Oxford might be obstructed or delayed as a result of the car driver having to weave his way through a clutter of dead academics which litter the roads.

In point of fact Glasgow is a huge sprawling but friendly place and the majority of ivy-covered Oxbridge professors are a shade too unworldly to be Moriarty-type figures. In fact it is said of some that one would need a second opinion to determine whether they were still alive. I've taken almost two hundred words to come to the point of my criticism but now I've finally arrived. Some months before my coronary Barry Cockcroft of Yorkshire Television had started making a documentary programme which sought to depict me as a man alone, facing the hardship and privations of a wilderness. When he contacted me a second time a few months after my coronary he was only too aware that he was speaking to a man who was reliant on medication and the carry over effect of intensive care in order to stay alive.

My encounter with Cockcroft, arguably the world's most furiously energetic man, was the result of an amazing coincidence. I was in the process of building a gypsy vardo – a bow-topped caravan – at the time and had chanced on a wonderfully illustrated book called *Romany Summer* on the shelves of W. H. Smith. The book shop owes me no favours I suppose, as for many years I would visit the shop, read a portion of a book every day immediately after school, replacing the volume on the shelf after a half hour or so of scanning the pages until I had finished the book. I rarely bought a book, I must confess, but I read a great many books courtesy of W. H. Smith over the years I spent in Lichfield. However, one day I chanced on a copy of Cockcroft's *Romany Summer* and was about to indulge in the process of reading a chapter a day when a shopper next to me nudged my arm. I turned to see a rather sallow skinned, wild eyed man of perhaps fifty clutching a copy of a gardening book. 'Has it struck you,' he began, a hint of pure venom in his voice, 'that a flower is the plant's sexual organ and at gardening shows plants are required to stand in vases of water while people gaze into their genitalia.' Quite clearly the poor fellow was bats and had a bee in his bonnet about plant rights. I was about to humour him and indulge in a game of drive the fool further when I noticed his particularly strong build and the particularly wild look in his eyes and thought better of my course of action, for I was never a brave man. 'Do something about it mate,' I muttered and added, 'I'll sign the petition,' before hurrying off, book in hand. Indeed there are some very strange people in this world and for some curious reason I seem to attract them. Indeed minutes after boarding a bus some lunatic will sit next to me and engage me in a furious argument about Fry's Chocolate Cream. Anyway, the upshot of the matter was that some of the shop assistants had seen me leap away, book in hand from the plant rights lunatic and in order to save face I subsequently bought the book.

Romany Summer is a well penned, well produced book about a documentary film made by Barry Cockcroft which was about the wanderings of one Cocker Smith, an itinerant Romany, and halfway through my reading the book, the telephone rang. By an amazing coincidence my caller was Barry Cockcroft who was investigating the possibility of a programme concerning my bizarre interest in rats.

Two years previously, Michael Croucher, a producer from BBC2, had filmed the events in a week in my chaotic lifestyle, the most memorable portion of which had been a Thursday night rat hunt using four of my terriers and half a dozen of my ratting team. Cockcroft, with his love of the bizarre and the macabre, had found the hunt fascinating and had decided to make a thirty minute documentary about my ratting experiences.

Alas the best laid plans of rats and men (sorry Robbie) aft gang aglae, for my ratting farm had closed and my ratting pack had been reduced by the death of geriatric terriers. Hence Cockcroft sought other ratting places for filming, but such places were hard to locate (the public health regulations saw to that) and the second filming of rat hunting was a little less than satisfactory – and that dear reader is magnificent meiosis.

Cockcroft cut short the filming for there simply was not enough film footage to make up a 45 minute programme, and shortly after the initial filming I experienced a coronary. Cockcroft is however skilled at the acrobatics of programme producing and shortly before the filming of the rat hunt, I had casually mentioned that I was interested in training a team of German Shepherd Dogs to pull sleds. It had been a casual comment, a spur of the moment statement, but Cockcroft had seized on the subject and used it to save the programme. Barry spoke with such energy and enthusiasm that I became even more aware of my frail physical condition.

There is a tale from Greek mythology of a man called Sisyphus who was foolish enough to divulge divine secrets to his fellow man. As a punishment for his folly, coupled with the fact that he had shown some reluctance about dying, The Judge Of The Dead condemned him to roll a huge block of stone up the brow of a hill and topple it down the farther slope. The catch was that Sisyphus was cursed never to complete his task, for before he succeeded in rolling the stone to the summit he was forced back by the weight of the stone, which rolled to the foot of the hill once again. I knew exactly how Sisyphus felt each day when I attempted to roll out of bed and start my day's chores, for every muscle ached, and every fibre of my being complained about the way I had abused my body during my youth. What was worse was that my current lady who had accompanied me on my trek from Lichfield, was a dynamic, if rather fey twenty-eight-year-old psychologist and the contrast between us made me feel even more depressed. My life had been spent wise cracking, joking about my inability to settle in the teaching profession and my many failed relationships with women. Now I felt I had lost my sense of humour and, on reflection, I rather pitied my youthful companion for the misery she had endured during her stay with me. God knows she found little about which to enthuse during her brief spell with me.

That evening I telephoned a doctor cousin and asked whether the making of a film of this nature was a possibility under the circumstances. She seemed amazed that I was even contemplating the venture and added, 'Wouldn't you need snow to complete such an enterprise, and is there the possibility that you would be required to work in very low temperatures or, even worse still, at high altitudes,' she didn't wait for a reply, 'I would say you needed advice from a psychiatrist rather than from a cardiologist,' and I suppose in my heart of hearts I knew she was correct. She continued in a clinical manner, 'You have just survived a coronary, the intensity of which is usually only revealed by autopsy and you are attempting a venture which would tax the stamina of a marathon runner of half your age,' she rang off, in disgust perhaps, leaving me to contemplate the future.

In coronary care I had met the ebullient Mr Matthews, a man with an amazing philosophy. Mr Matthews had suffered three coronaries and survived to be able to advise me. One day he sat by my bed when I was experiencing a particularly bad depression, 'There are two ways of dealing with a coronary, 'he suggested, 'One way is to go on with your life as if nothing has happened, the other is to wrap yourself up in cotton wool, avoid any stress, lead a sedentary life and virtually withdraw from the world. You may not live to see ninety, but if you adopt the second way of living, it will seem like it,' he joked. I reflected on his wisdom. My life had always been chaotic, disorganised and eccentric but never boring. Now trapped in a rather frail body for the first time in my life I was bored.

So it was that evening when Barry Cockcroft telephoned I agreed to do the programme, showing me breaking my German Shepherd Dog bitches to the sled on a high peak near Aviemore, where snow persisted until early May. I telephoned Steve Jones, my constant help during the last several years, immediately Barry had rung off and told him of my decision. Steve sighed softly and remarked somewhat dryly, 'Can I have your caned rocking chair (the only piece of property Steve coveted so it appeared) if you die during filming. I'll come with you,' he added – as I knew he would.

The more I know the more I realise how little I know, is an apt sort of epigram and when I considered the subject of training sled dogs, I began to realise just how little I actually did know. The truth was that despite the fact I knew all about the history of sled dogs, of the various breed which were used as sled dogs and the geography, geology and climatology of the Yukon, I had not the slightest idea of how to train and to couple a team of sled dogs. In short, I felt a little like a history don who specialised in the Punic Wars but was uncertain of the geographical position of Carthage.

The use of draught dogs had been forbidden in Britain since January 1st 1855 and there were many reasons for the passing of the act forbidding 'dog transport', as Lord Wicklow once described the use of dogs to transport goods and sometimes people. The use of dogs for draught work has been practised for hundreds of years by folk who were too poor to own horses or asses. Dr Caius, who published the fabulously inaccurate *De Canibus Britanicus* in 1570, mentions the patient tinker's dog – of no particular breed – which, loaded with solder, irons and tools, accompanied his master wherever trade dictated.

During the first Crusade, Robert, the rebellious son of William the Conqueror, used dog trains to transport goods and armour when an unknown illness saw off the horses, donkeys and mules during his trip across Europe but it was not the cheapness of draught dogs that attracted hauliers. Bristol sherry makers, who produced the famous Bristol Milk, the precursor of Bristol Cream, employed the services of large dogs – Newfoundlands were the most popular, for the breed had a reputation for great strength and small appetites – to haul crates and barrels of sherry, for the streets were so undermined with sherry and wine cellars that a dray and horses once fell through the road into a storage vault.

The fish delivery run from Southampton to London was often accomplished by dint of using heavy draught dogs. Two pairs of heavy mastiffs or Newfoundland dogs pulled a weight of three hundredweight of fish plus driver. Now lest the practice seems inordinately cruel, it should be pointed out that if a four-wheeled rig is kept well maintained and the wheels well oiled, a medium sized dog experiences little difficulty in hauling 200lb of freight. However, the lot of the draught dog was not always enviable. Robert Batson, a prominent member of the Society for the Prevention of Cruelty to Animals (the Society had not yet received Royal patronage), brought a private prosecution in 1836 against a haulier who kept his dogs in disgusting conditions and allowed the dog harnesses to chafe the animals until their shoulders were masses of bloody sores. After the Lambeth magistrates inspected these crossbred mastiffs and found them to be half starved, they sentenced the owner to fourteen days imprisonment, and one of the animals was so ill and injured that the court ordered that the wretched brute be destroyed.

Of course, not every haulier or owner of 'transport dogs', as Batson referred to the animals, was an inhuman brute. Captain M. E. Haworth, who published the curious little book *Road Scrapings* in 1882, tells of a legless cripple, Old Lal, who built himself a low slung carriage which was drawn by four foxhounds which he drove at 12 miles per hour. His team would have done credit to the kennel management of Hugo Meynell and slept beside and under Old Lal's wagon. After an eight mile run Old Lal would uncouple them and allow them to forage amongst the hog bins. 'Sometimes,' Haworth wrote rather sentimentally, ' he would even buy food for his dogs.' Now, in case the reader should decide to label Old Lal a brute, and a mean uncaring brute at that, it should be remembered that before Spratt devised and sold dog cakes (ship's biscuits impregnated with horse or knacker's meat), few owners fed their dogs properly and the animals were allowed to forage amongst waste food which was destined to be fed to pigs.

Yet it was not the supposed cruelty to the dogs that brought about the cessation of the use of draught dogs on the Queen's Highway. In 1838 a committee was appointed to investigate the increased incidence of hydrophobia, or rabies, in the city of London. It would be some years before Pasteur published findings concerning the effect of germs on organisms and cultures, and the majority of the public believed that dogs which were overworked 'spontaneously' developed rabies.

So it was in 1839 that a Metropolitan Police Act decreed that anyone using dogs for draught work were committing an offence and could be fined up to 40 shillings, and up to £5 for committing subsequent offences of the same nature. Two pounds was an incredible fine to pay at that time when a labourer would earn shillings not pounds for a week's hard work. So in 1855 it became illegal to use dogs for draught purposes on the Queen's Highway anywhere in the country, but it is still permissible to train dogs to pull carts etc. on private roads.

However, I was concerned with breaking my German Shepherd Dogs to the sled, not with training them to pull carts full of fish or sherry, and the object which sled-dogs pull is called a sled, not a sledge (which is a type of hammer) nor a sleigh, which is a carriage fitted with runners and is pulled by horses or, in exceptional cases, reindeer.

The runners of a modern sled are made of a hard, tough plastic material which with proper maintenance, will last for many years. During Jack London's day gold seekers 'shod' the runners with steel bands and these need regular maintenance to keep them running properly. The natives of Alaska and the Yukon had not entered the Iron Age when the Russians (who first colonised Alaska) encountered them. Yet they devised an ingenious method of constructing runners. Seal hides were bound together with sinews and then shaped until they formed serviceable runners. They were then thrust into sea water for a few moments. The runners froze until they were virtually as hard as iron and would last an entire winter. When spring came and the runners melted to form a stinking mess of putrid hide and hair the ever-hungry dogs ate the putrefying mess. Indeed, Eskimo dogs were famed for their ability to digest any food no matter how nauseating it may appear to human observers. Caius (1570) wrote disparagingly about Eskimo dogs and their omnivorous qualities, stating that they ate candles! Caius was an academic who knew little of dogs. Most of the candles of the poor of the time were made of mutton fat or tallow, only the very rich burned beeswax candles, and few British dogs would find such fare unacceptable. Yet Caius' contempt for those not fortunate enough to be British was typical of his times. The people who owned these candle eating dogs were referred to, rather contemptuously as Esquimaux, eaters of raw meat, by Europeans and held in little esteem by those who listened to the strange tales related about them by those who had journeyed into the Arctic. Yet no race is more attuned to a ferociously hostile environment than the Inuit, the proper name for these dwellers of a frozen north as indeed early Arctic explorers were to realise when they endeavoured to survive the rigours of an Arctic winter.

Dogs were harnessed to the sled by quite elaborate contraptions. Each dog wore a harness which fitted fairly snugly over the shoulders and back thereby allowing the dog to pull a great weight in relative comfort. A central line connected the sled to the lead dog and the other dogs were harnessed to various points on the lead line. London never quite mastered the social structure of the dog team and indicated that the lead dog would be the strongest and most ferocious member of the group. In point of fact, the most powerful dogs of a team are the wheel dogs, which are stationed directly in front of the sled, for these are required to bear the weight of the loaded vehicle when it is moving fluidly. Lead dogs are usually the brightest rather than the strongest members of the dog team and are required to know the words Gee (right turn), Haw (Left turn) and Mush (let's go) when working a trail.

What London didn't understand and few people do, I'm afraid, is that no dog will break trail – I'll explain the term. Dogs need to follow an already broken trail and will not break a trail through virgin snow unaided. If for some curious reason a trail comes to an abrupt end on a field of virgin snow, the dogs too come to an abrupt halt as though baffled as to what to do next. Early explorers travelled in pairs when running a team of dogs – one walking ahead to break a trail, the other handling the sled and controlling the dogs. Captain Howarth was amazed at the fact that some dogs pulled carriages and rigs for sixty miles a day, but on well broken, well packed, well frozen trails Arctic dogs pulled up to 200lb a piece for sometimes a hundred miles a day, sleeping deep, dreamless sleeps in dens dug in the snow.

Of course such dogs needed to be fed well to maintain such a lifestyle and the food needed to be of high calorific value with an adequate supply of protein to repair damaged muscle tissue. The dogs were fed on sun dried cod or salmon by their Inuit owners and large quantities of fat were added to the diet to raise the calorific value of the feed. A primitive, unscientific diet perhaps but when sled dog expert George Attla ran his dogs in the Iditarod, a 1,600 mile ordeal rather than a race, his dogs lost condition quite rapidly on the proprietary complete sled-dog food he was paid to endorse. Attla was dismayed at this loss of body weight and added fatty beaver meat to the diet to raise the quality.

Yet there is some evidence to suggest that even the Arctic sled dogs were badly nourished. Greenland is policed by some twenty five police/soldiers who travel vast distances using strains of native Eskimo dogs. These Danish troops are referred to as the Sirius Patrol and the sled dogs Sirius dogs for obvious reasons. In fifty years selection and good feeding has produced a bigger, stronger healthier, more tenacious animal than the native husky-type dogs which spawned the strain.

However, my own German Shepherd Dogs were not required to pull heavy loads over great distances but merely required to run two or three miles in deep snow in Aviemore. Yet at that time I had not the slightest notion how to train a team of German Shepherd Dogs to run in front of a sled, let alone run the incredible distances sled-dogs were reputed to run. However, my problems were to be solved by the incredible Cathy Rooney, personal assistant to Barry Cockcroft. Personal assistants or ladies with similar jobs but somewhat different names often run organisations. Indeed I have known schools where the staff were of the lowest possible calibre and where the head appeared to have sustained a lobotomy, literally stay afloat because the school secretary knew her job and was adept at covering up mistakes made by the teaching staff.

Cathy is one of those people who may not have an encyclopaedic knowledge, but, given only a brief period of time, could find out about any subject a person could imagine. She contacted me on a Wednesday morning and I confessed my total ignorance of the practical aspects of running a team of sled dogs. Surprisingly she seemed not the least perplexed that I knew nothing of sleds and sled dog management, and a day later the lady had found me not only a person who could teach me how to manage a team, but one who was prepared to take two weeks off work and help with the production of the programme.

John Evans kept, raced and bred Siberian huskies and for those not au fait with the subject of Siberian huskies, a brief account of the breed now follows. When the prospect of a fortune to be had at the diggings encouraged men of all races to journey north to the Yukon they sought to acquire large, powerful dogs capable of carrying quantities of freight north to the Klondyke gold fields. The fact that these dogs weren't particularly fleet of foot mattered little, providing they were capable of pulling at least 200lb of freight. In fact a prospector cum entrepreneur called Treadwell Walden bred a specially strong freighting dog, called the Chinook, to pull heavy sleds in the Yukon.

However, it wasn't long before sledding started to become a sporting event and racers sought out smaller, more fleet breeds of sled dog to compete in short races. An ideal sled dog was found just across the Bering Straits in Asia, where nomadic hunting tribes had perfected the breeding of a small, fleet sled dog, which today is known as the Siberian husky.

Now, despite the fact that these Siberian huskies are some of the most beautiful dogs in the world and have a certain wild look which endears them to lovers of the exotic, they are not everyone's choice of dog. The breed is wildly recalcitrant and difficult to control when off a leash. Furthermore, the Siberian husky has a justifiably bad reputation as a sheep worrier. In fact, should a Siberian husky escape from its kennels it is good policy to seek out the nearest field where sheep are kept. It is a racing certainty that the escaped husky will have also sought out and found the sheep – with devastating results.

Some years after I arrived in Caithness a young man who owned some Siberian huskies arrived in a village some eight miles from my own croft. His dogs were kept pegged out near their sleeping quarters but within sight of sheep. Each day I watched the dogs display what can only be described as an unwholesome enthusiasm as they watched their would-be victims, but newcomers to dogdom are invariably unwilling to take advice and it was only a matter of time until tragedy struck. One day two of the dogs somehow slipped their collars and wrought havoc on the sheep in the field adjacent to the kennels. In minutes the dogs had caused several thousand pounds worth of damage and I believe the young man left the county rather than pay for the damage the dogs had wrought.

How beautiful Evans' dogs appeared, and how very different from my own obedient, subservient and utterly tractable German Shepherd Dogs. Indeed it was quite understandable that Lorenz considered that the two breeds (Siberian huskies and German Shepherd Dogs) were descended from very different species of wild dog. Lorenz believed that the spitz-type dogs such as chow chows, astiaks, laikas, Siberian huskies were descended from the palearctic wolves (although this doesn't explain the curled tail of the spitz breeds) whereas collies, German Shepherd Dogs and other subservient breeds were descended from the golden jackal, a subservient, scavenging type of wild dog, frequently found feeding on the midden piles in Indian villages.

Lorenz might be forgiven for his heresy, for the two types of dog are so very different. Evans' Siberians had that natural, almost feral, look and lived only to pull. Off the leash they became laws unto themselves and while they obviously heard Evans' commands and possibly understood them, they chose to disregard his entreaties. Indoors they would clamber over Evans, giving displays of wild affection, licking him, lying on his lap and behaving in the ingratiating manner of a toy dog. Out of doors they did exactly as they pleased and declined, rather than refused, to come to hand.

My own German Shepherd Dogs clung to my heels, ignoring the antics of the Siberian huskies and when I moved, they too moved and it must have appeared as though they were welded to my sides. Later this clinging attitude, this reluctance to stray too far from my heels was to prove a hindrance when I finally broke them to the sled.

By dint of my contact with John Evans, I learned just enough to be able to break my first team of German Shepherd Dogs to the sled. In the years to come I was to break many teams of all kinds of breeds and once to engage in a rather humiliating race, pitting a team of eight bearded collies against a team of well trained Siberian huskies, but my first attempt at breaking a team has to be the most difficult, simply because of the fact my dogs had been taught to stay at heel – and I feel it is necessary to explain this statement forthwith.

Sled dogs, or non arctic breeds which are destined to be trained as sled dogs, go through a rather special early training programme. As soon as they have been inoculated they are subjected to a rather unusual lead training programme, for unlike the majority of pet dogs those dogs destined to be trained for sled dog work are required to pull mightily on the leash rather than walk quietly and meekly to heel. Some malemutes, huge, powerful, husky-type dogs, are trained to pull so hard that by dint of lunging they can snap an inch thick sisal rope. Out at exercise they test the arm strength of a weight lifter and it is said that Roger Mugford devised that ugly piece of equipment, the Halti, so that quite a small person could be able to control a dog with the pulling strength of a malemute. Those training Siberian huskies are also pulled along at a brisk rate by their wards and it is customary for sled dog handlers to reward (or perhaps simply allow) dogs to pull mightily on the lead when out at exercise. Thus when a sled dog is finally harnessed up it automatically pulls out in front and hence pulls the sled or rig.

Polly and her four daughters walked at heel. Perhaps I had overdone the obedience training for they clung like limpets to my side, never walking ahead, never considering running in front of me. I once walked along a crowded Birmingham street with Polly, Bimbo and Felicity off the lead and walking to heel, and perhaps, just perhaps, my actions smacked of ostentation but I was really proud of the control I had over them. Thus, when harnessed and asked to pull ahead they seemed baffled and even tried to turn in harness to walk to heel.

I watched Barry Cockcroft's face as the team attempted to turn about to walk behind me resulting in the sled and harness becoming a tangled mess. Cockcroft cast his eyes skywards, for he knew nothing about the ways of dogs, any dogs, and had expected instant success when the dogs were coupled. In point of fact at this stage in the film, I too was doubtful if the team could be taught to run in harness in the brief period of time we had to complete the filming. My lungs burned like fire as the temperature plummeted to below -25 degrees of frost and the altitude began to play havoc with my constitution. My chest pains had returned and the telltale ache in my upper left arm alerted me to the fact that I was far from well. I was decidedly ill and no longer had the necessary charisma to control a team of dogs – but there was worse to follow.

Steve patiently unpicked the tangle and once more harnessed up the German Shepherd Dogs, this time linking up John Evans' Siberian huskies as front runners to the team. Both had those frightening wall eyes – white, apparently sightless eyes which seem to terrify anyone who has no knowledge of the peculiarity. They looked such fearsome animals, a single step away from their palearctic lupine ancestors, able to revert to furious atavisms capable of eating my team of placid German Shepherd Dogs alive.

In the turmoil and tumult of the day, the chaos of my first attempt of harnessing the team, I overlooked the most obvious of mistakes I was about to make. I cannot offer any excuse for my stupidity, other than I was exhausted and unwell, but I allowed the most stupid of blunders to take place. During my course studying the training of circus dogs under Marie Stoka in Paris, and my spell at the Hartz attack dog training school, I had observed how a kennel of sane, sensible dogs could be disrupted by the appearance of a newcomer, an incoming dog with a strange scent. I had observed how toy dogs had been disrupted by what Steiniger had called intraspecific interfamily aggression. Yet, madness of madness, I allowed a pair of strange dogs to be harnessed alongside my own German Shepherd Dogs and had not anticipated the outcome of the action.

I had not long to wait before I realised the error of my ways. As John Evans' two huskies set off at a brisk trot, thereby encouraging my own dogs Polly, Felicity, Pagan and Beltane to move forward, towing the sled, I observed Felicity, the most docile of dogs, cast angry glances at Evans' Siberian huskies, but even then I was not wise enough to stop the training programme and allow the dogs to simmer down. Of course my team pulled, they had little option to do otherwise, with John Evans' wild-eyed Siberians pulling on in front, but once the team was uncoupled Polly, my docile, gentle Polly, Felicity and the very subservient Beltane set about the hyperactive Pagan with a vengeance. The television programme showed only rather silly skirmish but in reality the battle was much more serious, particularly as the wretched bitch, bound by her harness was unable to escape her attackers.

I raced to intercept the battle and, fortunately, Steve had also sensed the danger so there was little damage – physical damage – inflicted on Pagan. My anorak was, however, slashed asunder when it receive a panic induced bite from Pagan and it was only then that the television crew began to realise the awesome biting power of a German Shepherd Dog. The German Shepherd Dog team had been the petted, spoilt, easy going lapdogs until the incident but now cameramen and crew alike treated them with a new respect.

However, the incident did present problems regarding kennelling for the next few nights. After a fairly serious kennel fight it is policy to watch the warring participants for several nights after the battle, particularly if the dogs are kennelled together. Dogs and bitches which have become 'provocative victims' are aware of their plight and will sometimes display a desperate reluctance to enter a kennel alongside hostile kennel mates. Our position was, in fact, fairly desperate, for while in transit our German Shepherd Dogs were kennelled in a 30 cwt van.

Steve selflessly volunteered to sleep in the van alongside the dogs to prevent further damage to the wretched Pagan, but the owners of the Coylumbridge Hotel, where the film crew were lodged, finally agreed to allowing Steve and I to keep the dogs in our hotel room.

So it was that each night we returned to our hotel and slept with the dogs in our bedroom. Polly, Bimbo (who steadfastly refused to pull a sled despite her great strength), Felicity, and the now terrified Pagan, enjoyed an uneasy truce, a sort of peace enforced by Steve, for I was too exhausted to attempt to control the team. My doctor, a close personal friend, had warned that to attempt filming in high altitudes in temperatures well below freezing was little short of madness, and I realised he was correct. Each night I felt savage pains in my chest and left upper arms – a sure sign that I was not well, and I toppled into bed to experience a dreamless sleep.

By the tenth day of filming my dogs had accepted the harness and the fact they were required to pull a sled. I believe Bimbo enjoyed the work and seemed pleased to see the harness each morning. Polly and Felicity endured the position of wheel dogs, pulling directly in front of the sled and hence taking most of my weight phlegmatically but experiencing little pleasure in the activity.

London had written that when the goldrush in Yukon had started hundreds of large dogs were stolen from homes throughout the United States and Canada and broken to the sled, but while such dogs endured the privations of the trail few must have enjoyed an alien lifestyle pulling sleds in arctic conditions. Therefore when filming had finished I promised Polly and co. not to subject them to such an ordeal ever again – and, of course, I broke my promise to them.

CHAPTER 14

Life in the Highlands

'In the future everyone will be famous for fifteen minutes,' said Andy Warhol, whose statements were considered to be a little silly at the time he made them. Well, I had experienced my fifteen minutes of fame – a forty five minute programme as it happened – and returned to impoverished obscurity once the programme had been shown. I took stock of my situation immediately after the glitz and glamour of being a television star had subsided and my life couldn't have been more grim.

I had gone north with a young, vivacious divorcee some twenty years my junior. She was of the opinion that the man she had met was a self confident, man-against-the-wilderness type, she had read of in my books. My coronary and that television show had done much to dispel any faith she had in me, for I was now a prematurely aged man living on a pittance of a pension. I owned a small three and a half acre croft incapable of supporting me and, what was worse, the effort of getting out of bed in the morning exhausted me for the rest of the day. Friends kept regaling me with tales of recipients of heart attacks who changed their lifestyles and ran good times in the London Marathon, but I knew such activities were well beyond me. I was approaching a senile fifty and acted as would a man some twenty years older so there was little doubt as to why she tired of the lifestyle and left, leaving me to patch together a somewhat broken way of life.

Winters in Scotland are invariably harsh and at the 'Edge Of The World', as the artist Romy Brough referred to my home, life was desperately tough once November slipped and slithered into December. Torrential rain heralded the coming of my first real Christmas in the Highlands and my yard turned into the sort of slimy ooze one finds at the bottom of stagnant ponds. Each day I waded forth to feed and water the stock, only to return and render my living room awash with mud. My forays to fetch the mail from the post-box one-and-a-half miles distance left me exhausted and ill and each day as I waded down the water-filled lane I felt an ever worsening sense of hopelessness.

The New Year, a time when drunkenness increases tenfold in a county already saturated with alcohol, saw me staying indoors in an attempt to avoid meeting people, but my lifestyle was interrupted somewhat when a car pulled up in my yard and the village drunk – a hotly contested title in the district I'm afraid – rolled out onto the mud shouting and swearing as he did so. 'I'll kill you, Jock,' he screamed and, despite some deft footwork on my part, he managed to seize my hand and bite it to the bone, breaking my thumb like matchwood. He was helplessly drunk and, despite his diminutive size, incredibly strong and struggled violently with the police who came to fetch him. They explained that some three weeks before the said drunk had savaged a taxi driver's ankles and had been taken to 'dry out' in the local mental hospital. Clearly the drying out process had not been exactly successful for in his drunken rage he had virtually destroyed my door in an attempt to attack me.

By the time the police had arrived he had sobered somewhat and had become a snarling, growling beast, cowering in the corner of my living room, sobbing piteously between spells of curses and execrations. I refrained from making a complaint against him, for as a new lad on the block, so to speak, I could ill afford making my self unpopular in the tiny hamlet. It transpired that in his drunkenness he had mistaken my lane for that of a man he suspected of having an affair with his wife and had attacked me in error. However, the hilarity of Hogmanay aside, the encounter left me with a badly bitten hand and a thumb that dangled at an obscene angle. I cursed my ill luck at not having Polly indoors at the time of the attack but on reflection Polly would have probably killed my attacker and a dead, lacerated drunk would be difficult to explain even in a laissez-faire district like Caithness. So it was, I bound up my hand, set my thumb somewhat badly and began to prepare for the New Year, but if I tell the truth, never have I been more depressed at the prospect of the future and never have I been closer to suicide.

My hand festered badly, for the drunk had bitten with the fury of a bull terrier and I suspected that my low spirits would have accounted for the body's failure to allow my hand to heal. My diary took on the nature of an Edgar Allen Poe novel as despair was replaced by deeper depression. Romy telephoned early in January and on hearing of my plight offered to come and stay for a while until I healed. She added, leaving Hope squeaking rather feebly in the bottom of Pandora's box, 'Cheer up, the fine weather will see a host of new women in your life, Bri,' but the future looked decidedly bleak and grim.

It is quite amazing how we take the human thumb for granted and only when the digit is rendered hors de combat do we appreciate just how useful it is. As the Roman Empire drew to a close in the fifth century AD soldiers avoided conscription by amputating their thumbs and now, with my own strapped up to allow it to heal, I realised how incapacitating an injury to the thumb could be. It normally took me a full hour to clean out my dogs and barrow the soiled shavings to the bonfire. With my present injury I started cleaning at 10am, when it became light enough to see outside, and finished by mid-afternoon. My hand continued to fester despite the homespun nostrums I applied to the wound and eventually I was forced to visit Dr Frazer for antibiotics. He gazed at the suppurating mess and shook his head in despair, 'You value your life so little, don't you,' he uttered as he cleaned the wound and bandaged the festering wound. 'A bite from a human being is likely to fester anyway,' he explained and elaborated on the bacilli introduced by dint of human saliva. I was later to discover that my body's inability to cope with the infection was due to diabetes, another gift conferred on my by my coronary.

Spring arrived quite suddenly and so did Romy Brough. One morning as I paddled down the lane to fetch the post I noticed the geese moving north again, heading perhaps for Orkney and possibly farther north. Amongst the mail was a letter from Romy, written on one of her floral note sheets, stating that she was coming north with her children to help me for a week or so. I felt elated for I hadn't spoken to a soul since the encounter with my doctor and now felt in great need of human companionship. My telephone had been cut off due to the fact that I had been unable to pay the bill, and Romy had therefore written to me, offering her services as cook, housekeeper and nurse for a week or so.

'Oh, Bri,' she uttered, almost tearfully as she came through the front doorway. 'You really mustn't live like this. The house is so bare and devoid of human comforts that it's small wonder you are so depressed,' she continued, and set to trying to make my lifestyle a little more bearable. It was scarcely a holiday for Romy and her children, Tabitha and Christian, but when they left I felt they had done so much to alleviate my depression and heal my body. So it was that April found me more cheerful if not totally invigorated.

Spring in the Highlands is a furious time of year when Highlanders and incomers alike seem to come to life and the fields and moorlands abound with frenzied activity. The land enjoys only a short growing period so at the end of April, when frosts are less likely, potatoes and vegetables are planted, for most crofters grow their own vegetables, simply because by the time fresh vegetables are brought from the south they are no longer fresh. For those with no land to grow vegetables the shops offer vintage carrots, too long at the fair lettuce and senile Granny Smiths, hence it is expedient to grow one's own crops rather than exist on vegetables which give little or no nourishment.

That spring, Judy Umek, an American ex-girlfriend, sent me a somewhat belated book published by ISDRA – the International Sled Dog Racing Association, (or so I believe) which not only indicated how sled dogs could be trained but was also illustrated with line drawings showing Manitoba peasant farmers ploughing with dog teams. I telephoned Steve immediately, asking how such a plough might be made and promptly sent his drawings to a Thurso blacksmith to have the contraption constructed. A simple dog plough appeared within a week and once more I harnessed up the very reluctant sled dog team. It is possible to plough land using such a team, but only if the land has been previously broken up by a plough pulled by heavy horses or by tractors. Virgin turf is virtually impossible to plough with a dog sled, even one pulled by a strong and willing team of dogs, so after an exhausting and fruitless two weeks of trying to plough the wiry turf, I abandoned the project, leaving the expensive dog plough to rust in the corner of the barn and my spirits plummeted yet again.

There was, however, little time for depression as the short cool spring raced on towards a hot, dry summer, for the peat had yet to be cut. For those not conversant with the subject of peat cutting perhaps it's best to explain. Certain crofts, quite distinct from small farms found in England, have deeds which entitle crofters to go to the hill (every uncultivated area is known as 'the hill' in Caithness, despite the fact the county is flat and hill-less), and cut peat for fuel. Peat is the result of perhaps half a million years of decay of sedges and marsh trees, such as birch and alder, and is found some two feet or so below soil, though the best peat, the most combustible peat, is found considerably deeper.

Peat cutting can be attempted with a spade. Indeed in my early peat cutting days I used a spade to cut blocks some five inches thick. However, a real Highlander, a real died-in-the-wool sort, uses a wooden spatula with a blade some three feet long to cut peat, though the effort of cutting blocks of this size and lifting them to shoulder level so that the block can dry on top of the heather, is a Herculean feat, for such blocks when really sodden with marsh water weigh as much as eighty pounds.

However, lifted such blocks must be, if they are to dry for the winter and, hence, cutting begins in late April or May so that the pale summer sun and incessant summer winds can dry the peat. Peat blocks weighing 60lb when wet-cut will dry to form pitiful 4lb peats which burn rapidly and give off a fraction of the heat of the same amount of bituminous coal.

Peat ash is a very fine and invasive dust, usually pink, which covers persons and property within the house. At the time I went to Caithness I owned a cheap dust proof and waterproof watch which during my spell in Lichfield was regularly doused in mud and animal excrement. Yet the cheap watch, a present from one of my Godchildren, kept perfect time. Within three years of my coming to Caithness the watch stopped. It would have been easier to scrap the timepiece rather than repair it, but the wristwatch had sentimental value, besides which I dislike the ethics of a throwaway economy. Therefore, I visited a local watchmaker to have the watch repaired. He looked at the watch, shook it a few times and then unscrewed the back allowing the pale pink dust within the watch to spill out. He charged me a nominal £1 fee but suggested that I opened the watch each year to tip out the peat dust.

However, the chemical constituents and thermal value of peat aside, the cutting of this fuel is a nightmarish business. Seasoned peat cutters can cut enough peat to last a year in a single weekend (burning the peat on two fires which are lit throughout the winter and never allowed to extinguish until late May). Two people accomplish this miracle, one cutting and lifting, the other spreading the peat on the heather and moorland sedge to allow it to dry. However, to cut and spread peat single-handed is an exhausting task and one I knew I would find some difficulty in accomplishing. The television sledding incident had made me only too aware of my own shortcomings and the thought of another coronary in the middle of a lonely moor, my cadaver only discovered when the dogs began to wander from my corpse, terrified me. Yet I was determined to cut peat and save the £1,200 a year I was spending on coal. So it was I made a resolution to cut a hundred blocks of peat a day, spreading the blocks atop of the heather before leaving for home. My spirit was willing but my flesh was still so damnably weak. After cutting some fifty blocks, each weighing perhaps only 20lb, I fell exhausted against the sides of the peatcut and slipped into a deep coma-like sleep, to be awakened a full two hours later by Polly anxiously licking my face. I took some time to awaken and remember where I was, but once I attempted to climb out of the peatcut – a hole some eight feet deep – my muscles seized and I literally crawled the hundred or so yards home. I was desperately unfit but aware that my only way back to good health would be through exercise and open air living. That night I soaked in hot water until I was able to stand upright and next day I attempted another stint on the moor.

At the time I envied the lot of Polly, Bimbo, Beltane, Felicity and even the terrified Pagan, for while I laboured in the hole, the dogs sunned themselves on the heather seldom leaving my side to go off foraging. They had been joined by the Bimbo look-alike Eve who had an obsession for licking anything she found, be it organic or inorganic. A dead gull was licked avidly, as were decaying jellyfish and once I found her vomiting copiously, her sides heaving with the exertion of the exercise, after she had licked a toad. Toads secrete a poison called bufotalin, a toxin said to be one of the most bitter naturally occurring substances. Years before I had bred a demonic terrier called Vampire and such was his nature that he regularly killed toads, frothing and vomiting to expel the bitter bufotalin from his mouth, yet crazily attacking toads whenever he encountered them. Yet Eve had no desire to kill any creature. She simply desired to lick them. Once I found her licking a very tiny curlew chick, wet with saliva and wide-eyed with fear, yet unharmed by its encounter with the infantile Eve. Curiously Eve's sycophantic gestures were later to take her to the very brink of death.

As the summer progressed and the peats began to dry and shrink, I increased my work output to one hundred and fifty blocks a day, but by August I became only too aware of the pitiful quantity of peat I had cut. The peatcut adjacent to mine, cut with a flachter not a spade I must add, boasted a full quarter of an acre of neatly cut peat blocks spread across the moor. My own cut had produced only a quarter of this quantity of peat despite the fact that I had laboured for nearly three months and endured the torture of the damned, choking with chest pains, my skin eaten with midges. My neighbour had cut and spread a quarter of an acre of thick dry shiny black peat which was the result of a single weekend's work, his wife spreading the heavy blocks as he lifted them out of the peatcut.

I no longer live in Caithness but a few weeks ago I journeyed north for business reasons. My peatcut, unused for two or so years, now measures 100 yards long by 20 yards wide but I will always remember the first agonising 2 yard wide trench I cut across the moorland and the dogs which lay on the moor as I cut the peats. Polly watched as I toiled and laboured, sweated and cursed, throughout that long summer, questioning my sanity perhaps but never leaving my side. Later I would harness her to a makeshift pram-wheeled trolley to haul my badly shaped peats home and she did so without complaint.

The air above the moorland seethed with midges, that on certain days hung like a thick, black curtain. It was impossible to work under such conditions and I did my work shortly after dawn to avoid the savage biting these bloodsucking insects inflicted. I was merely irritated by the incessant biting but friends were more seriously affected by the attentions of the midges. One, a large, fleshy man, was bitten so badly that his face swelled up to elephantine proportions while his body resembled the carcass of Job after the curse of the boils. It took weeks for the wounds inflicted by the midges to subside and his flesh to clear of sores, after which he vowed never to return to the north.

A bleak and wet July gave rise to a sizzling August that brought out the adders and midges in number. Mey hill, the uncultivated land near my cottage was a herpetologist's haven, for the land abounded with adders. On the way to the peatcuts it was in fact expedient to watch where one trod because of the superabundance of the snakes. They seldom caused harm and when they bit a sheep, a horse or a store bullock the locals treated the bites in a most casual manner, lancing the blue-black swellings to allow the poisoned blood to flow before treating the bite with bicarbonate of soda. Polly avoided them almost instinctively while Bimbo and Felicity kept well clear of them. Eve, however, the inveterate licker, was virtually destined to encounter one.

Polly and I had walked up the hill on a blistering hot day in August, Bimbo and Felicity in attendance while Eve and the rest of the dogs exercised in the concrete run below us. It was a baking hot day, a day when the incessant wind had ceased and had attracted billions of midges, which hung some five feet above the ground waiting for some warm blooded creature to pass beneath them. I had long since ceased to use the lemon scented midge repellents and now silently endured the discomfort of the bites.

As I approached the peatcut I heard the heart-rending scream of a dog from the run below me and raced down to see what was amiss. I found Eve standing in the centre of the run furiously pawing her mouth. On examination I found the telltale two-holed puncture on her tongue, an organ which was swelling rapidly and threatening to cut off Eve's air supply.

Clearly an adder had bitten her and I found the culprit crawling away on the far side of the run but my immediate concern was Eve, who stood there wide-eyed with panic. I suspect that the gentle Eve had found the snake sunning itself in the run, attracted perhaps by the warmth of the concrete and, as was her way, she had attempted to lick the creature. However, the scenario of the incident was less important than the sight of the tongue which had taken on a blue-black colour and was now as large as a woman's fist. Legally I suppose I should have set off for the veterinary surgeon's, some sixteen miles distant, for it is illegal to perform the operation I was about to. I dragged the stupefied Eve out of the run and, using a sharp instrument, slashed her tongue. Her screams went up to Heaven and a dark spurt of blood drenched my clothes. If I might defend my action, which incidentally contravened the 1912 (Scotland) Protection Of Animals Act, I still believe that Eve would have choked to death long before I arrived in Thurso. Furthermore, I know that the veterinary surgeon did not keep a stock of anti-venom in his surgery. Eve panicked and raced around the yard and it took perhaps ten minutes to catch her and drag her indoors to reduce the possibility of death through shock. By late evening the swelling had almost subsided though the tongue remained blue-black and painful to touch for another week or so.

The bone-dry August faded into an equally dry September and it was time to haul home the peat on the home-made trolley designed by Steve Jones. Polly joyfully accepted the harness and willingly hauled the peat home across the bone-dry moor. So attached to me had she become that when I harnessed up Felicity, to give the now ageing Polly a rest, she became resentful of her daughter and began to menace her until finally I gave way and allowed Polly to haul the blocks of peat. Each trolley load weighed 40lb or so and she found it relatively easy to pull such a weight. Yet long before the first day was over I became aware Polly was no longer a young bitch. It is quite sad, but almost inevitable, that a person who enjoys a close relationship with a dog often fails to notice indications that the animal is ageing until the dog becomes almost geriatric. It is of course ludicrous to believe that one year of a dog's life is equal to seven of a man's, for bitches come in season and are ready for breeding at nine months of age and few girls are able to conceive on their fifth birthday, but at seven a German Shepherd Dog is past its best in some respects. The Abbess Juliana Berner of Sopwell Abbey once wrote of a greyhound – 'but when he as come to his seventh year then get to a tanner' (sell his skin to make gloves and falconry equipment) but the thought of putting the now ageing Polly to sleep was unthinkable and now as I reflect on the time, I realise she had many more useful years to offer me. Yet on the day we carted the peat home both Polly and I felt, and possibly looked, our ages.

Peat can either be stored under cover, but dry peat burns a little too quickly to be economical, or stacked in elaborately constructed pyramids, each construction containing the broken peat crumbs while the outside walls of the pyramid are built of the unbroken peat blocks. Many Highlanders take a great pride in the construction of their pyramids, even building the structures in the manner of elaborate bricklayer's bonds. My own pyramid was alas a ramshackle affair of which no one could be proud. The blocks were of dissimilar sizes and the volume of crumbs within the stack too great to be contained by the unbroken blocks.

My feeble attempts, my summer of toil and torture, had come to such 'little measure' and the peat had been burned long before the New Year. On reflection, however, I realised that I had regained at least some of my health and I felt it was time to start living again.

Chapter 15

The Boat

Hazel Cashmore, the Caithnessian beauty and artist, once said that if one survived the first winter in Caithness a person would never return to a life south of the Scottish Borders. My first winter had been a depressing time, a time when I felt that the world had little to offer me and I had even less to offer the world. Now with a renewed feeling of good health I set out to face the second winter.

If the first winter was harsh the second winter was more harsh. In November a calm serene day suddenly gave way to an icy gale which swept the land, tearing loose the tiles and sending galvanised sheets flying. The gale lasted five days and heralded in winter. Temperatures fell to below zero and stayed below zero for almost two months. Long before the two months had elapsed, the constant fires had burned out the peat pile leaving me to beachcomb for driftwood. Polly took great pleasure carrying strands of beachwood from the low-water mark to my wheelbarrow and it was almost as if she believed she was helping me in my quest for kindling. The truth was that Polly enjoyed retrieving for she had been rewarded for displaying an interest in the activity when she was still a puppy. Yet she displayed a strange perspicacity I have seldom seen in other dogs. One day, while beachcombing Mey beach, some eight hundred yards from my home, I spied a broken oar which I considered to be suitable for burning and in the nature of an idle gesture rather than an attempt at training I threw a pebble at the oar and bade Polly fetch it. Of course, she searched the sand and returned the pebble I had thrown, as indeed she had done so many times in the past. I laughed and shook my head, finally seeking out the oar, hurling it and sending her to fetch the object. She raced to the broken oar as gleefully as would a puppy and I praised her for her efforts. A few moments later I spied a broken wooden fish box (the sort which is meant to contain eight stone of fish, for fish is weighed by the box) and once again threw a pebble, striking the box with a smack. Polly watched my face, staring at me intently as if to try and understand my thinking, before setting off and retrieving the fish box to hand. I have in my kennels many of her grandchildren and even a great grandchild, many of which have won well in trials. Not one has displayed her strange perspicacity.

We beachcombed regularly throughout that winter, particularly after a high tide had cast a variety of flotsam on the high water mark. Most of the rubbish consisted of broken buoys, plastic floats and the battered remains of creels, smashed and twisted by the rough seas, but just now and again strange objects appeared. That winter I came upon the broken prow of a large boat, probably a boat smashed in an harbour, but who knows which harbour saw the sinking of the boat, for driftwood can travel hundreds of miles before being beached on some headland. Once I found a crate the writing on which was Cyrillic but this did not automatically mean that the crate had been washed westwards from Russia, for many Russian boats appear in the Pentland Firth and merchant sailors are exceedingly careless about the way they dispose of rubbish.

So it was that by dint of seeking out driftwood and examining maritime waste that I became interested in the sea. I have always had a terror of deep water, particularly deep, dark water, and my dreams are filled with horrendous visions of sinking in dark, deep pools in the depths of which lurk sucking insects and ferocious lamprey-like fish – work on that one Sigmund! Thus it was all the more puzzling to my friends when I decided to approach my bank manager with a view to buying a 16 foot fibreglass Orkney longliner, an easily repaired replicate clinker designed boat which was specifically tailored for the hostile waters of the Pentland Firth. My tiny boat was powered by an equally tiny eight horsepower engine which was capable of 6 knots on slack water – slightly better than a fast walking pace.

The Pentland Firth is one of the most feared stretches of sea in the world, hardly the place to start one's nautical career and is quite simply a narrow East to West sea passage which links the North Sea and the Atlantic Ocean. Tides which move from East to West and West to East therefore meet a bottleneck created by the proximity of the Orkney and the mainland Caithness and thus create fearsome currents which race up and down the Pentland Firth. The year before I left, a particularly high sea, coupled with an equally furious current, cast a tanker, the Betina Daniker, up onto the rocks of the island of Stroma where it remained

despite the efforts of salvage crews. Three years later the same conditions lifted the tanker from it's perch and sent it to the deeps.

It was hardly the stretch of water on which to learn seamanship, particularly as I had no experience of sailing or of boats. If I stop to think about it is in fact all the more baffling why I took to the sea for my food, as indeed I did for the next eight years. The only reason I can offer for my choice was perhaps that I considered myself incapable of drowning for I believe I am destined for a far more horrid form of death. Curiously enough, while at grammar school one of our teachers uttered what might have been a prophetic and justifiable statement (for I was a singularly odious sort of child), 'Plummer,' he would declare, 'You will never die by drowning. You are born to hang,' but I was to test the truth of his predictions to the full long before I left Caithness.

On the subject of drowning, there are many superstitions concerning death at sea that are still believed in Caithness. Children born with cauls, the remains of the amnion and chorion which buffer a foetus against the accidents and bumps to which the mother is subjected, are said never to die at sea. Perhaps the fact that these children enter the world still bathed in amniotic fluid probably has something to do with this belief. Yet despite the fact that drowning is an ever present danger for the Caithnessian seafarer, few sailors ever learn to swim. One of the coast guards, a rustic savant called John Green, once explained that waters around the coast which are chilled by Arctic currents are so cold that the life expectancy of a man cast overboard is minutes, even if a man can swim. Hence it is more logical for a person who finds himself in such a situation to wish to drown quickly rather than endure perhaps twelve minutes in icy waters before death through exposure, rather than by drowning, puts an end to his life. On a more macabre note, I met many men who were later to drown – which makes it all the more remarkable that a man such as myself, a man with little or no knowledge of the sea, survived eight hectic and dangerous years in Caithness. God knows, my ignorance and stupidity made it all the more surprising that I did not drown in those savage waters between Caithness and Orkney.

While I respect the rights of anyone who wishes to take out a boat and merely sail around the coastal waters, such an activity would not interest me. The sea offered me a sort of living, a chance to indulge in a sort of self sufficiency though the coastal waters had been raped and pillaged long before I arrived in Caithness. Thus it was that I resolved to take my food from those dangerous waters, though I confess I had never before caught a fish in my life.

However, shortly after I arrived in Caithness, while I was still unsteady on my feet and suffered from chest pains, I met a lighthouse keeper called David Noble, a native of Edinburgh who had decided to live a lonely life at the edge of the world. He had served his time as a chef, a ship's cook, and finally settled for the life of a lighthouse keeper. The job provided a house and just enough of an income to support wife and family. He had never earned large sums of money and if he wanted an object he attempted to make it.

Creels, or lobster pots, were made from hoops of an alkathene pipe and fish boxes, the covering netting of which was woven from some rough type of string. If he found an object on the beach he sought to adapt it for his personal use. Wooden fish boxes were regarded as treasures and he constructed many useful implements from the wood. When he learned I had a boat and no experience of how to use the craft, he threw in with me and made a fleet of creels for our common use. Polly who was by nature a little stand-offish with strangers took to David and his wife instantly and greeted both cordially when they arrived at my croft, and now I suppose it behoves me to explain what a creel is and how this curious piece of equipment works.

Bateman, an authority on various sorts of traps, states that man is nature's great imitator or copier, for virtually every trap is a development or an improvement on designs found in nature. Snares are simply an adaptation of lianas and vines that sometimes trap animals and birds in the tendrils of their foliage. Nets are merely copies of the webs of spiders, and creels are developments of objects into which fish or crustaceans found their way in but were unable to find their way out.

A simple creel consists of two hoops set in a solid floor and the hoops are then covered with netting into which a small hole is cut. A piece of fish is then suspended in the middle of the creel and the contraption lowered into the sea. In theory, at least, a crab or lobster senses the fish within the creel and attempts to find a way into the trap. When it does, it feeds on the bait and then is too stupid to find its way out. Thus when the creel is withdrawn from the water, usually once a day in waters where crabs and lobsters are not particularly numerous, an unfortunate crustacean is found trapped within the creel. Sometimes fish, young red cod, dogfish and the fearsome conger eel finds its way into the creel only to become bait or food for the creeler. Sometimes an octopus creeps into the trap to attack an unfortunate lobster within the creel and, like a creature from the pages of a Bram Stoker novel, injects a fluid into the lobster, an enzyme which turns the lobster's organs and flesh to liquid, and then sucks out the liquefied flesh from within the lobster's shell. Creelers despise octopi, partly because of their unwholesome appearance and partly because the creatures are so destructive to lobsters. I shall not relate the methods fishermen use to destroy octopi they find in the creels, sufficient to say the death of these creatures is far from pleasant.

In order to find such creels after they have been cast into the deep fishermen attach a buoy to the creel, joining buoy to creel with a length of thick rope. Plastic or nylon ropes are favoured today simply because they do not rot even after years of immersion in salt water. The buoys are usually made of plastic but during my beachcombing days along the Caithness shores I came upon two glass buoys of the type now found only in seaside curiosity shops today. How these glass buoys survived the buffeting of sea upon rocks, an action which smashes plastic buoys asunder, is a mystery but survive some of them have, for two now decorate a shelf in my home.

Crabs are enticed into creels by fresh fish only and if the fish is slightly tainted few crabs will be attracted to the bait. Lobsters are not such discerning creatures and long after fish have passed their prime the bait will still attract them. Readers who imagine that such creatures are overpriced should remember that the best lobsters are caught off very dangerous reefs, rocks into which the creeler must sail in order to retrieve his creels and during my stay in Caithness three creeler friends of mine came to grief in the dangerous waters which cover the jagged slate beds of the Pentland Firth.

Overpriced crustaceans – not a bit of it. During my last week in Caithness lobsters fetched nearly £3 a pound. Crabs, prime, good sized crabs fetched £2.75 a stone, two pounds seventy five pence for fourteen pounds of crab, slightly more that the cost of bait and to catch such crabs a creeler must work a day, sometimes in freezing conditions, sometimes in dangerous waters. True, at one time it was possible to catch huge hauls of crabs during a day's fishing but man has raped the sea as he has pillaged the land and now great hauls of brown crab are rare. The French however have a fancy for velvet crabs, tiny, downy crabs which are caught and ground to powder for the use of continental gourmets, though there is precious little meat on the bodies and claws of these tiny crabs. Crab buyers pay 25p a piece for such crabs and, for the time being at least, such crabs are numerous in the Pentland Firth.

I made little money fishing for crabs and lobsters in the shallow waters along the reefs of the Caithness shoreline but the activity gave me a new lease of life. For nearly a year I had lived the life of an invalid, existing, living what Thoreau called a half life, waiting perhaps for death to end the dreadful monotony of my existence. Now at last I found some excitement in my life and the excitement was made tenfold because of my ineptitude at seamanship. So many times I came within a hair's breadth of drowning, largely through bad seamanship and my ineptitude at handling a boat. I tangled amongst the creel ropes which criss-crossed the bay, put my tiny boat on the rocks at Mey bay during a particularly bad swell. Once while attempting to fetch in my creels in heavy fog I drifted out into the Firth into the path of a tanker. The wash of this giant boat nearly capsized me, yet somehow I managed to survive. Perhaps I had a guardian angel or perhaps my teacher was correct when he stated I was born to hang not to drown. Most of the local fishermen expected me to drown, for now that I had regained some of my health I began to indulge in a series of reckless acts which caused fellow creelers to question my sanity. Somehow I felt that a coronary, a flirting affair with death, was an indication that I had little time left and that I must live every moment to the full. Furthermore, my frequent encounters with near catastrophes and my escapes from these encounters gave me a curious feeling of being invulnerable. As this false feeling of confidence increased I began to take even more ridiculous risks, setting my creels amongst the most dangerous rocks along the reef. Once I sailed full tilt into the waters of Men of Mey, the most dangerous stretch of sea in Britain, a passage, the bottom of which is littered with the wrecks of larger boats which had been crewed by far more competent sailors that I will ever become. Yet somehow I seemed to survive the most outrageous of incidents and, madness of madness, as time went by I neglected to take my lifejacket to sea, leaving it to hang in my kennels. Once a cousin of mine, in true Don Juan style, attempted to seduce a nun so as to tempt the wrath of her husband (God). Now because of my belief in my own invulnerability I too tempted the Fates. As I write I reflect on the times and marvel at the fact I managed to survive my spell of creeling in the Pentland Firth.

One day I took Polly and Felicity to Thurso and visited the Seaman's Mission at Scrabster for lunch. Not only was the food served there good, plentiful and cheap but not one of the other diners objected to the fact that two large, powerful dogs accompanied me. The Mission was filled with sailors, fishermen from as far afield as the Faroe Islands, local creelers and maritime raconteurs who could spin magical tales of the sea. One, seeing Polly and Felicity, swayed across to me and introduced himself, remarking that during his spell in Canada he had owned similar type dogs called the Chinook. If the owner will forgive a slight digression I will explain what a Chinook is.

In the late 1890s a trader called Treadwell Walden realised that while the California goldrush of 1849 made men rich the Yukon strike was unlikely to recoup the money spent on the mining of gold. In fact the venture cost sixty million dollars but netted only sixteen million dollars worth of gold.

Walden, therefore, made a goodly sum by ferrying food and essential goods to the goldfields by dog team. Indeed he once bought a load of tin plated dog dishes which he sold in the Yukon as gold panning trays. One day when the prospectors began to sour of the goldrush Treadwell Walden traded a bag of flour for a fine sled dog – proof of how down on his luck the prospector was – which Treadwell Walden called Chinook after the warm Pacific breeze. From this sled dog he bred a strain of draught dogs which he called Chinooks.

My Canadian associate listened to my account of what a Chinook was before introducing himself. It transpired his name was Freddie Bartholomew but I refrained from mentioning the androgynous child actor of the same name, simply because the Canadian sailor was a huge hulk of a man and I am by nature a coward. Freddie had worked off St John's Bank, Newfoundland and had a wealth of seafaring tales to tell. Freddie must have been eighty at the time and related stories of the war in the Pacific where his merchant vessel had been torpedoes by Japanese submarines and he had drifted for a week, half-mad from lack of water and baked by an equatorial sun. He told tales of primitive Milesian tribesmen who indulged in cargo cult worship, deifying an American airman who parachuted to an island where the natives had yet to see a white man. 'There's a McDonalds restaurant on the island now,' he sneered rather regretting that a type of civilisation had reached the island.

What interested me most were his tales of fishing off St John's Bank for giant cod large enough to swallow a man's leg. What was even more interesting were his tales of boatdogs who worked between the flat-bottomed dories and the mother ships of the cod fleets.

Apparently despite the Englishman's reputation for being dog-mad, the French have always been more willing to use dogs for work. Tale has it that French sailors out from Newfoundland were wont to take huge mastiff type dogs, similar in type to Pyrenean Mountain Dogs, on fishing trips and these great dogs took messages between ships, killed huge cod – large enough to swallow Bartholomew's leg perhaps – and rescued drowning sailors. These dogs sometimes strayed to the mainland mated native curs and produced the Labrador retriever and its larger cousin the Newfoundland.

Newfoundlands are apparently tailor-made as boatdogs. They are strong, hardy and take to water like otters, coupled with which despite their great size they will live on the most frugal of diets. Early settlers kept them as draught dogs and fed them on a diet of fish scraps, cabbage and waste potatoes and, apparently, they thrived on this diet. Dogs fed on fish frequently develop a painful paralysis called Chastek's disease but apparently many years of privation has made the Newfoundland immune to such a disorder.

These dogs were trained to recover buoy ropes and thus assist sailors in hauling nets which had gone adrift, but apparently the sight of a man overboard motivated these dogs to swim out and try to save these drowning sailors. So strong was the instinct in these dogs that they were sometimes a nuisance. A lifesaving team working the banks of the Seine employed several Newfoundlands but the dogs were eventually dropped from the corps as they often swam out to save swimmers who were not in difficulty.

I listened spellbound to Bartholomew's tales and found that afternoon had slunk into evening so engrossed was I with the stories told by this elderly seaman. However, Bartholomew was an astute man and when he had finished his tales he commented, 'You are going to try out my stories on that dog aren't you,' and before allowing me to reply he added, 'Every time I've mentioned about dogs you keep fondling your bitch's ears!'

Of course he was correct, for such was my confidence in Polly and the reciprocity I shared with her that I felt there was nothing I could not teach her. In point of fact, training her to retrieve creel ropes was simplicity itself but then everything I decided to teach Polly was learned so quickly that I was amazed. It took only a day or so to accustom Polly to travelling in a boat and training proper began. I simply cut a length of creel rope – a ten inch piece – threw it and asked Polly to retrieve the rope. She did so instantly, as though amazed as to why I should want to test her intelligence with such a simple exercise. I then cast the length of rope into the water and bade Polly retrieve it. This she also did with ease. I then threw a six feet length of rope along the quay and this too Polly retrieved. I then attached a buoy to the rope and Polly fetched it to hand, bumping the buoy along the quay as she retrieved the rope buoy combination. The combination was then thrown into the water than this too Polly fetched to hand, swimming into the deep water like a seal.

Teaching her was so easy. In the 1950s a psychologist called Skinner stated that he could teach virtually any creature any skill simply by breaking down the activity into a series of simple steps and rewarding each step before proceeding to the next. He achieved amazing results to demonstrate his theory and I often wonder what a skilled trainer such as Skinner could have done with an animal with Polly's intelligence. She performed so well at every task I set her, despite the fact that her trainer was a world-weary tired old man who trained dogs simply to demonstrate his own vanity.

We set out to recover my creels from the reef that evening without waiting for high water to allow my boat to pass over very sharp rocks. I took a handful of stones in order to be able to throw them to direct Polly to the creels. She swam to the buoys, seized the rope attached to them and retrieved each creel rope to hand, thereby allowing me to haul the creels from the safety of deep water. That evening I caught only five small edible brown crabs in my twenty four creels, but I felt so wonderfully jubilant about the fact that I had, in a single afternoon, taught Polly to work from a boat. I am a simple man, one never concerned with a sybaritic lifestyle and I find pleasure in the most simple of successes. That evening I returned home swapping my crabs for duck eggs produced by a friendly neighbour and ate the eggs with broad beans I had grown in the garden behind the croft. I have seldom experienced such elation and at that point in my life I realised that Paul Getty was not as rich as I. Getty needed more money to maintain his lifestyle, whereas I had everything I needed. I have always tried to practice the lifestyle written of by Thoreau – a man is rich in proportion to what he can do without – and now I realised that the author of *Walden* was correct. My stomach was full of good, home-grown food, my house was heated with fuel I could cut on the moor and I had trained and worked the most splendid of dog. True, my clothes were, and still are, threadbare but I placed little value on the notion that clothes made the man. I had virtually everything I required.

It is a curious fact that once I achieve this sort of earthly Nirvana some unpleasant ailment infects me. Next morning I awoke with a sharp pain in my shoulder and by noon a huge boil had started to appear. I had always thought that God's test of Job's faith – inflicting him with boils – was a rather silly test of a man's willpower until, that is, I experienced such an affliction. By nightfall the shoulder and side of my neck were agony to touch, yet I knew that next day I needed to work quite hard weeding my potatoes, feeding my livestock and, agony of agonies, lifting my creels which were weighted down with some fifteen pounds of concrete. Morning found me in agony and a red inflamed patch spreading down my back. I fed the dogs, cleaned them but not properly and returned to bed, finding it difficult to find a comfortable position in which to sleep. Polly seemed to sense my pain and somehow – and I am possibly interpreting her behaviour in an anthropomorphic manner – adopted a doleful expression as if sympathising with my plight.

I rummaged through my medicine kit for some antique bottle of antibiotic but finding none, ransacked my kennel cabinet for Synolux, an augmented antibiotic which was capable of dealing with a staphylococcus infection, despite the fact the antibiotic was not recommended for human use. However, I took a large quantity of Synolux – enough to dose a large pig the label stated – but despite the fact that I continued with the treatment for the recommended seven days the swelling still remained and I felt decidedly ill. I am now aware that I am diabetic and diabetic patients are not only prone to staphylococcal infections but need special treatment in order to recover from such infections.

By the eighth day I felt as though I might die, for my temperature had risen and I began to vomit copiously. On that day the unstoppable Freddie Bartholomew arrived and saw my plight. Polly as usual greeted him with suspicion as she did with everyone who came to the house and her suspicion grew when Freddie began to manhandle me in order to see the extent of the infection. A sharp intake of breath from him indicated to me how far the infection had spread, but Freddie assured me he could treat it for he had seen many such infections during his spell at sea. On reflection I feel I must have been mad to allow him to treat me, but I felt so ill I didn't feel my lot could worsen. 'This isn't going to hurt, is it?' I asked, and added, 'I'm not very good at enduring pain,' but Freddie didn't reply and filled a bottle with water and began heating it on my peat fire, holding the bottle with a damp cloth while the water evaporated. When the bottle seemed empty, or at least free of liquid, he placed the hot vessel over the boil and to this day I can still feel the touch of the warm glass as he pressed it into my flesh.

As the glass began to cool I felt my flesh squeezed upwards as the infected area was seemingly sucked up the vacuum created by the evaporated steam and I felt the agony of the damned as this dreadful sucking sensation increased. I think, but I'm not sure, that something in my shoulders and neck exploded but I lapsed into unconsciousness so I can remember little of what happened. I awoke believing that I had experienced some form of fainting spell, only to find my clothes drenched with blood and Polly standing over the now terrified Freddie

Bartholomew. 'For God's sake get her off,' he whispered and Polly stood back as soon as I bade her do so. It transpired that just prior to my passing into unconsciousness I had screamed and Polly, believing that Freddie was hurting me, attacked him pinning him to the floor. For nearly twenty minutes she had stood over the terrified man growling into his face and wetting his clothes with slaver.

Freddie cleaned up the filth that had exploded from the boil with trembling hands and covered the wound with a dressing before leaving. True to his word I recovered, though the agony of the treatment will always be remembered. Sufficient to say Freddie never visited my house again, though he wrote sending me a Get Well card. Freddie died in London at his daughter's private nursing home only a year later. He was eighty-eight at the time of his demise and had been spared the trauma of senility until days before his death.

The summer moved on at a graceful pace until the time came when no more lobsters appeared in the creels. Around about July lobsters shed their skins, or shells, and for a while they are soft-shelled, naked and vulnerable. In this condition they are reluctant to venture forth to feed and lie up in crevasses in the rocks until their shells harden. At this time of year creelers, full time, not amateur meddlers like myself, lift and dry equipment and repair damage to ropes and creels.

The same week as I lifted my own small fleet of creels I received a letter from a young man called Neil Mackie who had read one of my books and wrote offering me some ferrets. What was of greater importance, however, was the fact that Neil mentioned that he owned a small fishing boat and worked gill nets in Aberdeen. To cut quite a long story short, Neil arrived bringing with him a gill net, and for the rest of that summer I fished for cod, pollack, wrasse and coalfish to fill my deep freezer – a piece of second-hand equipment given me by a local farmer who seemingly took pity on my state of penury.

Now creeling is quite a simple operation, particularly if one knows the lie of the seabed and where to drop one's creels. Gill netting is a little more complicated – well for a person with my limited manual skills anyway – and if the fisherman is uncertain of what he is doing can finish up as quite a dangerous occupation. A gill net may be any length, the Japanese fish with three mile nets, mine was a hundred yards long and some six feet deep. The net is weighted by a bottom lead line and kept upright by a buoyant float. The net is cast into the sea across the tide that runs in an East-West West-East direction. Fish, borne by the tide, now become enmeshed in the apparatus and are hauled to the surface twice a day, an hour or so after the tides.

So it was, equipped with such a net, I set to sea at a time when all good creelers were land-bound repairing their equipment. My catch varied considerably; one day my nets were laden with lesser spotted dog fish, tasteless fish with newt-like faces, which I froze down, fed to my stock until they sickened of fish and finally dug the remainder into my potato bed. The following year the leaves of the potatoes were a bright lambent green colour and the tubers beneath them waxy and huge. Long before the winter past I had sickened of the fish in the freezer and even my dogs refused to eat it.

Cod, rich red-gold cod, coloured by the kelp beds in the bay, were welcome additions to my diet, yet the locals refused to eat such coloured fish, which they believe to be worm ridden. Pollack, a close relative of the cod is also held in low esteem, possibly because the best pollack seem to congregate around sewage outlets and hence are known by the less than poetic name of Shitey Sarahs. Coalfish are also difficult to sell and the northern Scot, despite the fact he claims that everything that comes out of the sea is edible, will only contemplate eating haddock and plaice.

The net sometimes entrapped unwelcome visitors. Early in September I lengthened my buoy lines and went to fish in deeper waters. The catch now consisted of only coalfish, mackerel sized, half grown fish which were edible but not particularly appealing. I continued to hand-haul the heavy net while Polly watched me from the prow of the boat, fascinated by the still wriggling coalfish which fell from the meshes. One day something large was fighting in the bottom of the net, and I hauled the faster to recover the catch which I believed to be a very large silver cod, worth 80p a pound in the local hotel which specialised in selling freshly caught fish. I hauled the great fish to the surface only to find that I had netted a conger eel as long as my arm span and thick as a man's thigh.

Readers who have never encountered such fish are probably unaware of their terrible biting power. It was said that at one time the Ayrshire crofters went hunting such fish, which were trapped in rock pools at low tide, with bull terriers and that sometimes so fierce were the eels that they overmatched the fighting dogs. The bite of the conger is terrible and a tale will suffice to explain just how powerful the bite can be. A fisherman creeling out of John O'Groats found a medium sized conger eel curled up in his creel, attracted by the fish bait no doubt. The biter was to be bitten however, for the conger was released, its body chopped up and used for more bait, while its multi-toothed head was cast under the seat. An hour later the creeler arrived back in the harbour and began to clean out his boat. The disembodied head then bit him so savagely that it severed a portion of his thumb.

The creature entrapped in the meshes of my net was many times bigger and, without wishing to exaggerate, weighed in at perhaps a little less than 80lb, and as I pulled the net aboard the monster slipped out of the meshes. It was a fearsome brute and as I gazed at the cavernous multi-toothed maw and the lashing tail I though of the Midgard Serpent, a mythical eel-like beast that encircled the world, but I had little time to reflect on the Asgard Pantheon for the beast was thrashing around in the well of the boat, biting like a fiend. My net was half in the boat while the heavy anchoring weight clung to the bottom of the sea, hence it was impossible to return to the harbour, particularly as the brute lay between me and my tiny outboard motor. In such situations I resort to panic and for a moment or so contemplated abandoning the boat and swimming the two miles back to the harbour. I stood at the prow of the boat, desperately trying to avoid the huge, bull terrier sized head which I considered capable of biting off one of my hands, when Polly erupted and attacked the brute. Polly was quick but the huge fish was quicker and sank its teeth deeper into her shoulder, hanging on like a limpet as Polly bit furiously at the beast's body. German Shepherd Dogs are not particularly brave dogs and Polly often screamed with pain if I accidentally stepped on her foot or tail, but she bore the pain of the awesome bite in silence, and continued to savage the beast's body. For a while I watched the combat, a bizarre battle between a dog and a giant, oversized fish, mesmerised by a hybrid sense between fear and awe, but sensing that matters were not going Polly's way, I seized an oar and began to belabour the eel's slimy body. It was difficult to estimate how long the battle lasted, for the struggle seemed to continue for an eternity, but eventually Polly's shaking the fish and my battering the creature with an oar caused the conger to release its hold on Polly and I was able by dint of a Herculean effort to scoop the fish over the side of the boat and watch the monster return to the deep.

I fell desperately exhausted into the bottom of the boat, my breath hissing from my lungs, too tired to haul the rest of the net or to tend the terrible wound in Polly's shoulder, and it was a full hour before I recovered enough to lift my nets and sail back to the harbour. I neglected to untangle my catch and raced home to tend the very damaged Polly, who was by now beginning to look decidedly unwell. The bite had not removed a piece of flesh as I had hitherto thought but had crushed and macerated the shoulder muscles. Stitching was impossible for there was little of the muscle which could be drawn together, so I bathed and disinfected the wound as best I could. Polly looked dreadfully unwell and it was weeks before she could walk around the yard again. The wound became a large brown scab which fell clear of Polly's body in late September, leaving a bare shoulder which never furred over again.

I told my tale to Angus Bain, an Orcadian creeler, but Bain had a tale to cap the battle in the boat. 'When I was a young man,' he began, 'I creeled out between Stroma and Swona, two islands in the Pentland Firth, and it was my custom to take a collie dog such as that,' he pointed to the bearded collie, Dot, which lay unobtrusively under the chair, 'on the boat with me. I took her mainly for company,' he continued, 'for she would not face the water as your dog would – nor would she herd well,' he remarked rather wistfully before continuing with his tale. 'That year killer whales appeared in the Firth but caused little harm and became curiosities rather than menaces – until, that is', he remarked, 'I took my collie out on the boat. When I did, one black and white devil (a killer whale) followed the boat and attempted to jump up and seize the collie, eventually trying to bite the sides of the boat. I had never heard of a whale attacking a boat before or after this time,' he added leaving me to offer an explanation as to why the whale behaved as it did.

It is not, I believe, policy to offer any explanation of a maritime happening to any northern Scottish fisherman, for no southerner has an inkling of any event north of the border – or so it is believed by the Scots. In point of fact the attack on the boat was fairly easily explained. Lorenz, the behaviourist, remarks that very few animals possess the specialisation of retina that enables man to see a clearly defined picture. Thus the dog at the prow or stern of the vessel resembled a seal, the principal quarry of the killer whale. Whales are, however, able to see colour and hence the whales never seemed to attack a boat which carried a dog of unseal-like colour. I refrained from offering this explanation to Angus who was convinced that I, in common with most southerners, was mentally retarded and knew nothing.

Towards the end of October I had reason to believe the statement 'You are born to hang, Plummer for you'll never drown' may well have been true for until then I had not realised how dangerous my dabbling in the Pentland Firth had been. The lobsters were fading again and a few small, undersized youngsters had found their way into my creels. These lobsters are thrown back – I believe there is some law which prevents one from harvesting them, though truth to tell there are few laws which offer fish of any sort any sort of protection. Cod are often eviscerated alive or in good years crushed by the multitude of fish within the hold, but I digress and must find a way back to my tale.

Lobsters live within crevices in the rock, coming out to scavenge and hunt only after dark, unless, that is, they are voraciously hungry. So it was that I dropped my creels in Mey, a hundred yards from the Queen Mother's castle. The reef is extremely dangerous and consists of razor-edged slabs of slate, the beds of which are set at an angle so as to trap the unwary fisherman and gut his boat. I had little to fear however, for now armed with a catapult and a hundred or so pebbles I was able to stay offshore and cast a stone towards the creels before I bade Polly fetch the creel rope attached to the buoy. By doing so I placed myself in little danger and could easily haul creels at any time of the day, unlike the other creelers who had to wait until high water in order to haul their creels. On the day in question I had been warned about going out to fetch the creels for the very worst of sea scenarios was about to come together. A rocky coastline such as the one found on either side of the Pentland Firth is extremely dangerous but never more dangerous than when there is a strong sea wind which pushes any vessel towards the shore, and such a wind was not only blowing but the effect of wind coupled with a high tide would have been terrifying to any experienced, competent fisherman. However, I was inexperienced and a star's flight from being competent, so, against all advice, set out to fetch my creels.

An icy wind had started to blow from somewhere out in the North Atlantic and I can remember thinking that the long dry Indian summer had at last come to an end, for the seasons at these latitudes are sharply defined. However, both Polly and I shivered out to sea to fetch the creels. I shut off the engine and shot a pebble in the direction of the nearest creel buoy and, dutifully, Polly slid over the side to fetch the creel rope, but I was unaware that huge waves were building up out in the Pentland Firth and pushing me towards the jagged reef. It is always wise to post a lookout when a sea wind starts to blow. Indeed there is a tale of herring fishers fishing to the west of Thurso who unwisely continued to haul without a lookout and the entire small fleet paid for their folly with their lives. Equally unwisely I concentrated on watching Polly fetching the rope and was oblivious to the awful danger behind me. Polly swam with little effort, I must add, towards the buoy rope but at the last minute, just as she lifted the rope in her mouth, she vanished underneath a huge wave. A few seconds later she reappeared desperately struggling to swim towards me, creel rope still in her mouth, but another huge wave – the seventh wave of Caithnessian folklore perhaps – lifted her once again and flung her onto the sharp reef rocks.

Realising she was in difficulties I reached behind me to start up the outboard but try as I might, I could not start up the engine and, driven by the wind, I felt myself drawn as by a magnet to the sharp reef rocks. I have never been a brave man, a foolhardy man, perhaps, but never a brave one and I panicked. I set up the rowlocks in seconds and desperately tried to row away from the reef but the incoming tide and the sea wind made even my frenzied efforts futile, and, despite the fact that I rowed as I had never rowed before, I watched the jagged rocks of the reef coming closer and closer.

Polly had disappeared from view and I considered her drowned or perhaps smashed and bleeding, but nevertheless dead and lying in one of those deep rock pools which abound around the coast. A huge wave lifted me and I watched one of my oars floating away from the boat. My panic suddenly knew no bounds. The reef rocks were now only inches below my boat and I knew another seventh wave would surely smash me in two. I desperately reached for the outboard starter and pulled as though my life depended on the engine starting – as indeed it did – and my silent prayer was answered, for the 8 horsepower engine roared into life. I spun the boat round and headed back to the harbour where I knew it was unlikely I would find Polly alive.

It took me a full half-hour to travel the six hundred yards back to my mooring in Harrow. I moored my boat quickly, and badly I must add, before clambering up the ladder to the quay and racing off around the beach to seek for Polly. As I ran a dull ache suffused my chest and up into my jaw, but such was my frenzy in searching for Polly that I chose to disregard the warning signs. I ran for half a mile before I saw a dirty-white, kelp covered mound on the rocks and slithered and slid towards it. Miraculously Polly was still breathing, the creel rope inches from her mouth, and as I dragged her to the beach water belched forth from inside her. Polly weighed nearly 80lb, so to get her back to the car I rolled her body into an old fish box and attempted to pull her towards the harbour. Fortunately, just as I felt my breath burning the back of my throat and the dull ache creeping down my left, arm two ten-year-old boys saw my predicament and helped me haul poor Polly back to my shabby van. We loaded Polly and when I had recovered my breath I offered the lads a pound each for their troubles, only to be told they didn't accept money from strange men! I knew exactly what they meant as I felt there could be few stranger men in the county than me – a ragged, soaked man who was attempting to drag a half-drowned dog in a fish box.

Polly recovered slowly from her ordeal but it was days before she could stand and totter around the kitchen. The year had been a traumatic one for us both. She had been bitten badly, battered and nearly drowned, and I was still recovering from some form of blood poisoning, an after-effect of the curious boil and the even more curious witchcraft methods practised by Freddie Bartholomew.

I took stock of my situation once more; Polly was clearly hors de combat and winter was fast approaching, so there were few days left for me to creel the bay. One night while bathing I discovered that my athlete's foot, a complaint which had defied all known medical treatment, had suddenly vanished. Out of curiosity I telephoned my cousin who after a few years of general medical practice had decided to become a dermatologist. 'It's probably the effect of constant soaking in sea water and other unpleasant entities,' she remarked but added, probably aware of my hypochondria, 'It's curious though some parasitic fungi and worms tend to leave the organism if they suspect the host is about to die!'

The very next day I hauled my creels for the last time and drew my boat up the slipway onto the quay. For me the fishing year was over.

CHAPTER 16

Roly Pig

I drew my boat in October, running the outboard motor in a butt of rainwater to rinse the salt from the moving parts, and prepared to sit out the winter, which had duly arrived in November. The peat fires roared to ashes as the winds increased in velocity and the house became snug and warm. The walls of my croft, like the rest of the native built crofts, were a yard thick and the croft was set in a hollow as a protection against the constant winter wind. Indeed, two storey houses were once referred to as 'Englishman's houses' by the locals who realised the folly of building many storied houses which would groan and complain when the winter winds began to blow.

In windy conditions peat burns brightly and, alas, quickly and my pyramid of peat began to dwindle before Christmas arrived. Yet the house would become intensely hot on windy nights. One night the house became so swelteringly hot that I suspected a house fire. It transpired that the iron plate of the Aga cooker had become red hot, so hot in fact that it illuminated the room. Yet without such appliances the temperature in the croft was so terribly low. In fact when I made winter visits to the house prior to moving to Caithness, I slept in the fitted wardrobes in order to keep warm.

Part of the problem of living in Caithness is the fact the county is now treeless and thus the winter wind that originates in the Arctic wastes of Siberia is not buffered by the forests which once covered the county. At one time the land was covered by scrub oak, gnarled and twisted trees which supplied the Viking ship builders of Orkney with timber. Birch woodlands covered the marshy, uncultivated 'hill' and willow was once planted next to the croft houses. Not only did willow trees offer some, though not much, protection from the wind but the thin branches could be woven into some sort of lobster pot which, weighted with a stone, could be cast into the waters around the reef. I met a man called Robert MacKay in Dornoch who was an expert in antique Highland practices and he demonstrated how a willow lobster pot could be constructed from willow wands. By dint of knife and thin willow wands he created a functional though flimsy creel in minutes. Such creels would nevertheless last a season after which they could be left to the deep and other creels made the following year. Willow grows very rapidly. Indeed a Swedish breeder has produced a strain of willow which grows so rapidly that it can be used as fuel for power stations.

As the winter began to deepen the weather became more and more furious, as if defying outsiders such as myself to stay in the county. On January 4th I walked to the mailbox, wading through the deep puddles in the lane as I did so. Halfway to the box I was driven to seek shelter against a sheepstone (flat slabs of Dunnet slate set on edge to afford some protection for sheep wintering in the fields) by a hailstorm, which cast down hailstones large as marbles and left my face bruised and my left eye closed by the swelling. In 1920 there were tales of sheep killed by a storm which produced outsized hailstones, but then Caithness hosts many tales of freakish intermittent weather. Yet snow, really heavy deep snow, is rare in Caithness despite the fact that Thurso is 250 miles north of Moscow. However, as the winter continued to deepen, the omnipresent wind ceased one day and the heavens opened allowing two inches of snow to fall in a matter of three or four hours, cutting off the croft from the main road and increasing my sense of isolation and loneliness. I have never been a sociable person and rather enjoyed the title of odd-man-out in a crowd. Yet that winter I really craved human companionship of any kind and some days waited for the telephone to ring so that I might hear a human voice.

My stack of peat still remained, or rather, the small crumbs of the peat stack were still to be found under the snow, so each morning I harnessed Polly, together with her ebullient descendants Pagan and Beltane, and hauled the bags of frozen peat crumbs home to the croft. After the first leisurely day's haul I suddenly realised Polly looked decidedly tired and old. The autumn of inactivity had allowed her girth to increase considerably and her day's efforts left her exhausted. Two years previously she would have treated the hauls from the moor as something of a game – though Polly was a very serious sort of dog. Now she looked decidedly pained as I released her from her harness and allowed her to lie next to the Aga cooker where she slept.

Fortunately she was spared the problems of hip dysplasia, a problem which plagued many of her descendants. For those who are unaware of the problem, hip dysplasia is a badly fitting hip joint, a state where the head of the femur fits badly into the acetabelum of the pelvis and where joints fit badly, arthritis is quick to take hold. Thus, dysplastic animals suffer the agonies of the damned. Polly was never hip scored (low score good, high score bad) but unlike many modern dogs who lead cosseted puppyhoods so that they might achieve a low hip score at a year of age, Polly had led a terribly harsh and active life. There is a tale of a police dog who was hip scored at the age of seven and achieved a hip score of 64 – an acceptable hip score is 20 or less, one must add. Yet the dog had never shown the slightest indication of lameness and it was assumed that such was the quality of the muscles of the hind legs that the joint was kept in place by the muscle structure.

Modern breeders often go to extreme lengths to ensure a hip score is low and puppies are not allowed to over-exercise, are carried down stairs, lifted off settees all in an effort to prevent any future hip problems. Polly had never enjoyed such treatment and had leaped fences and walls, pulled heavy weights and swum great distances. Her hip score was probably very high, even as high as that of the police dog I've just mentioned, but I suspect that the iron hard muscles of her hind legs kept the joint in place. If she was ever in pain she never showed it but at night after a rigorous period she slept a deep, dreamless, deathlike sleep and was reluctant to wake at dawn when the day's work began again.

So it was I sat out that long and cold winter without seeing a single soul for nearly two months. I often found myself holding conversations with Polly, asking her far from rhetorical questions and requesting her silent consent on matters of kennel management, feeling a little like a crew-cut Ben Gunn perhaps, but unlike the said hermit I was in desperate need of human company. Romy telephoned less frequently, for her art work was now in great demand and I saw prints of her paintings of poppies for sale in art catalogues. Moses never telephoned and I suspect that in the hurly burly of a life overflowing with grandchildren he must have lost my telephone number.

Yet there was cause for greater gloom on the horizon. When the first days of spring appeared I mated three bitches in an effort to get money to repair the roof of my main kennel. The bitches became pregnant and went full-term but all the puppies died. Each bitch produced a lusty litter of ten large puppies but within a day or so their natural squeals degenerated into unhealthy croaks and the whole litter died.

When deaths of this nature occur it is essential to ascertain the cause of the problem, and autopsy revealed that the puppies had died of an E.Coli infection, an infection that is the very devil to clear from one's premises. How the bacteria had come to lodge in my kennels was a mystery, though I suspect that as my kennel was simply a converted cowshed, the disease was related to white scour, an ailment that kills calves.

The standard treatment for the disease is to clean the place thoroughly and leave the premises clear of any livestock for a full year to allow the bacteria to die off. However, my kennels were the only ones I had and hence I chose to adopt another policy. Some days before my next bitches were due to whelp I cleaned the kennels thoroughly to remove the grease produced by the dogs, from the kennel walls. Grease will host myriads of forms of bacteria and viruses and hence until it is removed, further sterilisation is futile. I removed the grease by scrubbing the walls with a hot, strong solution of washing soda which caused the grease to saponify – to turn to soap – which was then washed away with water. I had previously underestimated the caustic nature of plain old commonplace washing soda until the hot solution splashed on my face and hair. I ignored the splashes, only to find the skin on my cheeks peeling as though subjected to strong sunburn and patches of my hair parting company with my scalp.

Once the grease had been removed the whole building was then washed in a strong bleach solution and left to dry. The building took on the aroma of a public baths, but there was further sterilisation to follow. The kennel was then doused in clean water again and every niche and crevice in the building sealed. Once the building was rendered almost airtight a few pounds of purple potassium permanganate was stirred into a gallon or so of formaldehyde and the mixture stirred vigorously. I then raced outside, slamming the sealed door behind me while clouds of acrid vapour permeated every nook and cranny in the kennels, killing insects, mice and other denizens of the building. The kennel was then left for a full day for the vapour to disperse and the bitches then whelped in the sterile sheds. It is, of course, virtually impossible to kill the bacteria by dint of sterilisation of this nature, but it did provide a cleaner environment in which puppies could be born, even though the building needed similar treatment before each bitch started to whelp.

As a result of my treatment, my bitches produced three litters of live, lusty puppies which grew into large, powerful German Shepherd Dogs, although I failed to sell them. Such is the attitude of the Highlander that they believe that goods must be sold cheaply by incomers but not to incomers. A puppy advertised in Caithness for less than a reasonable price is regarded as far too expensive and the natives throw up their hands in horror uttering, 'You'll never get that price up here.' Yet petrol is dearer in the far reaches of the Highlands as is food, and local tradesmen charge incomers outlandish prices for their services. One incomer who wished to build a house found it cheaper to import labour from Glasgow and board them in bed and breakfast houses rather than to employ local labour. Whatever the cause of these peculiarities I found it impossible to sell my puppies and finally gave them away to friends in the south. I had many enquiries for the whelps when I placed an advert in the *John O'Groat's Journal* but once I spoke of the price the caller hissed, as though struck in the solar plexus by a sharp blow, before concluding the telephone call.

Occupied as I was with sterilisation and fumigation however, I nearly failed to notice that winter had slipped into a short spring and the fury and frenzy of potato planting and peat cutting was with me once more. I planted a full acre of potatoes, hiring a friendly neighbour to plough and sow my field and set to to cut my peat, this year trebling the quantity of peat I had cut previously. Each evening I returned home tired, but not sick and exhausted as I had felt the previous year, for clearly I had recovered from my coronary and had my diabetes under control. On May 7th I cut and hauled 704 blocks – a pitiful amount by local standard perhaps but enough to render my arms tired and my back aching.

The same day I slid my boat down the slipway in Harrow Harbour and set my nets, Polly sailing with me, gazing into the water at the swaying kelp fronds. I was reluctant to use her as a boatdog again because of her age and somewhat creaky condition but such was her enthusiasm as she watched me load my nets that I decided it was cruel to deny her the trip. That day I caught a large quantity of medium sized golden cod and some huge pollack which I froze for the summer but I felt some trepidation about fishing into the summer when my nets would yield a large quantity of useless, bland tasting, lesser spotted dogfish.

Work expands to fill the time available for its completion, or so says Northcote Parkinson. My own philosophy dictates that the amount of stock I keep is dictated by the supply of cheap food I can obtain. I had fed the last catch of dogfish to my dogs until the animals had refused to even sniff the sandpaper-hided miniature sharks, and then buried the remaining fish in a potato bed where five months later the stinking mess was still attracting flies and other creatures who were not averse to eating putrefying fish. Yet the sheer waste disgusted me. My philosophy, based somewhat loosely on that of Thoreau, dictated that if I killed an animal or bird I found a use for the creature. Indeed, even the rats I killed were fed to my ferrets. Now, however, I was catching several tons of low-grade but high protein fish and using it as fertiliser, and while I confess the potatoes I grew using dogfish as a manure developed the lustrous green foliage of plants described by Michael Moorcroft, and the tubers, free from the taints of chemical fertiliser, tasted quite different from shop bought potatoes, the loss of piscean life to grow such crops could not be justified. Early North American farmers ploughed tons of lovesick grunion to grow crops but this is an appalling misuse of living creatures. Rudolph Steiner, founder of a school of somewhat oblique but sound-thinking, would have disapproved of my uneconomical use of the fish protein and would have advocated feeding the protein to an animal which will tolerate piscean protein (and not all animals will, for mink, ferrets and dogs develop Chastek's paralysis if fed an overabundance of fish) and then utilised the dung passed by these animals to fertilise crops.

A little about dogfish before proceeding further, however. Dogfish are amongst the oldest denizens of the deep and appeared many millions of years before land dwelling beasts. In common with sharks and rays, dogfish are boneless. Ribs, spines, fins are not stiffened with calcareous material but are composed of cartilaginous matter, which is equally as efficient as bone. The livers of these fish are vitamin rich and the flesh, while virtually tasteless, is very high quality protein. Furthermore, the lesser spotted dogfish is extremely numerous in northern waters and quite large fish are found in creels and nets and are regarded as something of a nuisance by fishermen. Even as a bait the lesser spotted dogfish has its limitations. The flesh emits little scent to attract crabs and lobsters so if dogfish are to be used as bait it is usually mixed with strong scented fish such as mackerel. Crabs and lobsters then crawl into the creels, attracted by the fragments of mackerel and then spend hours tearing at the tasteless dogfish, thereby preventing the crustaceans escaping from the creels. Creelers regard dogfish as very second-rate bait. In fact during a huge glut when my nets yielded nearly two tons of dogfish in a week I attempted to sell the bait to creelers. Some refused it, some offered me 50p a box (112lb) if I delivered the fish to Scrabster and Wick harbour. It was in fact not worth my while setting nets and untangling the snakelike bodies from the nets for the pence I was offered for dogfish. Cod, prime net-caught large silver cod sold for £80 a box one should add, but no one wanted lesser spotted dogfish.

So it was that I determined to buy stock which would eat lesser spotted dogfish and possibly thrive on such a diet and the obvious, indeed the only, choice of animal was pigs.

The only breeder of pigs in the county were the MacLeod brothers who lived in a remote cottage at Lochend and kept a variety of crossbred white pigs, feeding them on a mixture of bruised barley (grains of barley split until the animals which are fed the barley can digest the nutritious barley kernel) and pig meal. Pigs fed such a low protein diet grow slowly and there is little profit in rearing such animals, particularly as pig keepers are not subsidised by agricultural grants. Pigs need a diet of roughly 18% utilisable protein to grow and barley contains only 10% protein. Therefore pigs fed such a diet take many months to reach killable weight. However, the flesh of dogfish is very rich in protein – the dried flesh contains 66% lysine and allied protein, and if fed in moderation, is an excellent pig food.

I took Polly to fetch the eight-week-old piglets from Lochend. She began to wag her tail in ecstasy when she savoured the scent of the piglets which the MacLeods had loaded into sacks. Clearly the aroma had awoken memories of poor Emma, the Duroc piglet Polly had suckled during my stay in Lichfield, but these were an entirely different matter. These hybrids had been reared with one goal in mind – the production of 200lb pigs suitable for pork rather than bacon production. They weighed perhaps 22lb and cost a pound a pound to buy as piglets, and were so suspicious of human beings (justly so perhaps) as to be as wild as hawks.

Polly watched them as I released them in their pens and in two days came into milk. We understand so little of canine behaviour but I suspect that distinctive porcine smell triggered off some endocrinal reaction in Polly, a reaction that brought about the production of milk. She tried her hardest to approach the piglets in order to clean them but they were terrified of her and raced to the far side of the pen. Yet Polly would not have her maternal qualities rejected and stayed outside the pen gazing in at them, wagging her tail as a gesture of affection. Indeed even as the pigs were eventually loaded for slaughter and weighed nearly 300lb Polly attempted to clean the backsides of the terrified beasts.

The pigs were quartered in a wooden sty set within an acre of land which was overgrown with thistles and twitch, the most unproductive piece of land imaginable. A half a century ago or maybe more someone had dumped a load of builders rubble on the plot and the passage of time had allowed the rubble to sink below the surface but, more disturbing still, adders slithered between the cracks in the rubble and produced live young in the builder's waste. Adders, unlike most snakes, are viviparous and produce live fully formed young, tiny perhaps but venomous nevertheless. They pose little threat to human beings and reports of human beings who have been bitten by adders usually indicate that for some reason the victims were usually barefooted or bare legged and accidentally stepped on the snakes. However, I felt some trepidation about allowing pigs to root and browse on land where adders abounded, though my fears were later found to be unjustified.

Within a week of their arrival the piglets had started to root out the weed growth in the field and to burrow down into the peaty soil to feed on the deep-rooted thistles and rushes. At first the rooting was superficial and barely two inches deep, but as the pigs grew larger they began to dig deeper into the mixture of rubble and peat until craters two feet deep appeared in the field. One day I found one of the young boars racing around the field, a live adder hanging from its mouth. At first I thought the actions of the piglet were due to the bite of the adder, for the poison often causes the victim to behave in an excited manner some minutes after the bite. The excitement, however, was due to the fact that the pigs regarded live adders as a luxury and once one pig rooted one out the rest chased it to snatch at the wretched snake. One day I watched one of the piglets pulling a huge two-and-a-half foot adder from its lair in the manner of a thrush extracting a worm, but never once did I find an adder bite on the snouts of the pigs. Could it be that pigs are immune to adder bites or does the thick hide which covers a pig's face prevent the venom reaching the capillaries beneath the hide?

That summer the pigs, fed on a witch's brew of dogfish boiled with potatoes, waste vegetables dried off with bruised barley, grew accordingly, for pigs are amazingly omnivorous. One day Polly and I chanced on a bed of comfrey growing near an abandoned croft house. Comfrey is reputedly the most amazing of crops and virtually anyone who has attempted a life of self-sufficiency has used the plant. Its leaves are high in protein and vitamins and it has the ability to extract valuable potash from deep in the subsoil. It also has medicinal properties and was at one time regarded as a cure-all. Hippocrates, the father of medicine, once advised that poultices of comfrey should be used to bind up broken bones, hence the plant's name Knitheal. Regardless of the plant's wonderful medicinal properties the pigs ate it voraciously, eating as much as ten pounds of comfrey apiece for five or six days.

Nothing I threw them was considered inedible. Once when my velvet crabs died in the creels – velvet crabs often die if confined in creels for a few days – I fed the crabs, shells and all to the pigs. They crunched up the shell a little and then swallowed the tiny crabs whole. Weaver fish, whose dorsal fins sport poisonous spines, were eaten with relish when cooked, though I had some trepidation about feeding the fish when I saw Neil Mackie's hand fester and take on the nature of a misshapen cactus plant when he was pricked by the dorsal fins of a weaver fish. Cooking apparently neutralises the poison or else kills the bacteria such spines carry. Octopus was rejected when raw, for such is the rubbery nature of the carcasses that pigs were reluctant to ingest them. However, when cooked, added to the seething witch's brew which boiled and bubbled from morning until night, the pigs wolfed down these eight-legged monstrosities.

It is almost amazing that anyone who has to buy commercially prepared pig food can make a profit from keeping pigs, such is the cost of meal and the quantity growing pigs will eat. That first summer the pigs cost me little to keep them, though I experienced a summer of drudgery and dirt, filling and stoking the boiler with peatcrumbs and driftwood. I was warned by locals, the majority of whom had never kept pigs, that pork from fish-fed animals had an incredibly fishy taint. Yet dogfish were so bland and tasteless that they imparted little or not taste to the meat. Once I found a dead seal on the beach, a half-grown male which had a rifle bullet hole in its head. Seals wreak havoc with the salmon nets which stretch across Dunnet Bay and hence fishermen shoot them without mercy. I sliced up the freshly killed cadaver and took the pungent meat home to feed the dogs but despite the fact my dogs had lived on meal for a full week, for there was a shortage of offal at the time, they refused to eat the seal meat. My pigs were less fastidious, for after I boiled the vile smelling flesh they accepted it graciously. In point of fact I was committing a serious offence feeding such fare to pigs, for according to the Diseases of Animals Act Order (Waste Food) 1973 it is illegal to feed any meat, bones, blood and offal to pigs, though I'm fairly certain that seal meat would not contain any bacteria harmful to pigs. Nevertheless, fines of £1,000 have been imposed on those who have sought to disregard this Act.

Summer once again slipped into autumn and the dogfish returned to the deep water, leaving only their egg cases, mermaids' purses as the locals called them, as a reminder of their visit and forcing me to feed pollack and seal meat to maintain the pigs. A week before slaughter I stopped preparing my toe of newt, eye of bat mixture and gave the beasts bruised barley to cleanse their systems. They dropped in condition at an alarming rate but not enough to dissuade the slaughterman from remarking that these were the best pigs that he had ever seen. Loading pigs on a cart prior to slaughter is a tricky business for pigs cannot be driven in the manner of sheep or cattle. Pigs have to be lured onboard with offerings of food, though I felt like a Judas tempting them onboard with a bucket of their beloved fish swill.

So it was, the fields were made fertile, the deep-rooted thistles removed by the grubbing action of the pigs and my broken down freezer filled with the meat of pigs – rough cut perhaps but edible nevertheless. All in all it had been a profitable but messy summer and I no longer felt guilty about the fact that I was catching and wasting virtually tons of dogfish. Furthermore, my experiment in self-sufficiency had rekindled my interest in pigs, an interest which had begun with the acquisition of the unfortunate Emma and I now decided that, once the pens had been cleaned and the land allowed to lose a little of its pig sickness (the build-up of some of the organisms which are detrimental to pigs) I should keep pigs once more – possibly one of the endangered breeds of pig.

I finally settled on Tamworth pigs, gingery-red pigs which were once popular with smallholders, for the breed had the ability to utilise all the waste vegetables a smallholder might produce. The breed grows slowly, for the Tamworth has been metabolically geared to existing on a poor diet, but the pork from such animals is truly excellent. Tamworths are hardy pigs – I was about to find out just how hardy the were the following winter – and hence they seemed ideally suited for the conditions in Caithness. So it was, I set out to find a breeder who kept these unusual red pigs and who was prepared to sell me a trio of tiny piglets. I finally found one south of Inverness and a week later I loaded Polly in the van and set out to fetch them.

How strange people are and how dictatorial are the ways of that most peculiar of mammalian forms – the 'man in the street'. I stopped off in Inverness partly because I was a little too early for my interview with the pig breeder and partly because I needed to eat – and I was learning to control my diabetes at the time. I sat on a bench near the river and allowed Polly to wander along the path a little, for she loved to savour the scent of strange dogs or possibly rabbits which were abundant in the Highlands that year. As I did so I observed a smartly dressed man approaching, or rather, bearing down on, me for I sensed his hostility long before he approached me. At first I thought he was antipathetic to the fact I had allowed Polly to wander off the lead, for these days people seem decidedly touchy about dogs of any breed which seem likely to foul in public places, but I was wrong about my antagonist, for such he proved to be, reason for approaching me. He stopped near my seat and pointing to Polly he divulged the reason for coming to see me. 'Do you realise that breeding those white Alsatians,' – he had obviously been out of touch with breeders of this type of dog for many years, for not since the 1970s had the breed been referred to as Alsatians – 'is immoral.' I glanced up and found the man to be one of those neatly dressed, slightly effeminate men my mother insisted on calling 'dapper'. 'Really,' I replied, seeking to avoid a confrontation with a man who clearly had a bee in his bonnet about the subject. 'Do you realise,' he continued, 'that German breeders are forced to put down any white puppies so as to prevent the breed from deteriorating.' I was about to reply that I could list several German customs which were far from desirable but thought better of it as the tiny man was puce with indignation. I suspected the man was a school teacher, for a man amongst children quickly degenerates into a child amongst men, and waited for his next comment. His outburst continued, 'I hope you aren't intending to breed from that, that abomination,' he pointed at Polly with the toe of his brightly polished shoe. He stood next to me almost puce with rage and I suspected that in addition to being a school teacher, he was also slightly mentally unstable. As he continued to rant and rave I reflected on what tiny incidents have caused major wars. The War Of Jenkin's Ear came to mind, an engagement triggered by the removal of an ear from an English sailor which created great hostility between England and Spain. Trivial matters often spark off major battles, particularly where dogs are concerned and it is by no means uncommon to find dog breeders – I shall refrain from using the term 'dog lovers' for obvious reasons – poisoning rival breeders' dogs when the said dogs had defeated the poisoners' dogs at a minor show.

To engage such a man in discussion would not only have been rather ridiculous but slightly dangerous for he had decidedly fixed views on the subject, so I remained silent lest I antagonise the man further. As he continued to rant and rave, uttering execrations concerning white German Shepherds and those who sought to breed them, I reflected on Polly's worth. She had served me so well, had taken part in every activity my grasshopper mind had decided I should try and never once questioned my judgement. She had been a delight to own, a positive treasure, charming with children, hostile with those who sought to harm me, a dog of a lifetime, in fact. My antagonist had now run out of words and stood before me, panting with rage and indignation. I allowed him to finish his furious diatribe and stood uttering, 'I see, I shall put her to sleep tomorrow,' before clicking my fingers and bringing Polly instantly to hand. Curiously I felt terribly treacherous about not defending my beloved Polly and slunk off towards my van. The last duel in Britain where Captain McNamara killed Colonel Montgomery was fought over a disagreement about Newfoundlands, so perhaps the approach I had decided to take was a wise one, and I drove off to Hoy to fetch my piglets.

The litter of Tamworth piglets were sired by a show champion and were in splendid condition, so without further ado I bought a trio, spending more that twice the amount I would have paid for some of MacLeod's crossbreeds, but I have never regretted the purchase. As I signed my cheque I watched Polly gazing lovingly through the bars of the pen and wagging her tail ecstatically. She was overjoyed at the fact that the tiny piglets stood nose to nose with her as interested in her as she was in them, and I knew this action augured well for the future.

However, in many ways Polly's maternal qualities did not augur well for her own future at least and eventually led to her decline. Within days of the arrival of the piglets Polly came into milk again and became extremely sluggish as her teats became swollen with the milk. Mammals which are unable to get rid of surplus milk are targets for the illness known as mastitis which occurs when a bacteria called staphylococcus aureus or staphylococcus pyogenes invades the mammary glands and at one time the disease was extremely serious. Early dog breeders dosed infected bitches with Epsom salts to decrease the bitch's milk flow but this did nothing to curb the infection. In fact it is quite difficult to treat a staphylococcus aureus infection with conventional antibiotics as the bacteria secretes an enzyme called penicillinase which negates the effect of penicillin and penicillin related antibiotics. Some of the modern proprietary antibiotics now contain potassium clarulante or clavunalic acid which slays penicillinase-making bacteria and allows the antibiotic to function properly. So it was that when I had treated Polly with Epsom salts and saw her scouring badly, I resorted to use of the augmented antibiotic Synulox (amoxycillin plus clavulanic acid) and this cleared the infection. Yet each day I found Polly gazing sadly at the piglets, inviting them to suckle her. She would eagerly clean their oversized hams and stand to allow them to take her milk but, unlike Emma, they declined her hospitality.

Winter arrived early with a sleet shower late in September and the icy weather indicated that it was time to haul my nets and creels and sit out the winter. Late in October I took Polly to the moor and harnessed her to the peat trolley but she was reluctant to pull the contraption. At one time I thought she had delighted in the activity for she became excited when I took down the sled harness. Now she seemed reluctant to allow me to harness her and moaned softly when I touched her. Some days she would be reluctant to leave her warm bed near the Aga cooker, though she still visited the pig field to gaze sadly at the fast growing trio of piglets who avoided her when she tried to clean them. Polly, alas, never learned to accept the fact that her attentions were unwanted and I had to watch constantly lest she came into milk again.

The Tamworth piglets were a very different kettle of fish from the white crossbred piglets I bought from MacLeods' at Lochend. If the commercial white pigs were omnivorous, the Tamworths were more so. Virtually any organic material was regarded as edible and they burrowed deeply in the weedy pasture for insects, worms and roots. Roly, the boar, dug furiously as if he hated the soil and one day I found him two feet deep in the earth, digging furiously into the stony subsoil to extract the tough thistle roots. The sows behaved impeccably and were so tame as to allow small children all manner of liberties with them. Roly was less so, though when half-grown he would allow me to straddle his back so that he might ferry me a few yards before shaking me off my perch. Pigs are so terribly strong and can be dangerous, if only because of their insatiable appetites and clumsy movements. One day Roly, seeing me carrying a bucket of food, rushed to greet me, stepping on my toes and shattering my toenails. The pain was excruciating and I needed to cut off my socks to ascertain the damage the great brute had done. A month later my badly smashed toenails fell from my feet, or rather peeled off with my socks.

What were more terrifying than Roly's great bulk were the tusks he began to develop when he reached six months-of-age. By the time Roly was eighteen months old these tusks had developed into six inch curved, bevelled daggers capable of inflicting terrible damage on any foe. Curiously, and certainly ominously, as the tusks began to develop, Roly's disposition began to change. No longer was he the copper-haired happy piglet who eagerly awaited feeding time, but a rather terrifying beast who watched my approach with a slyness that boded evil.

A boars' tusks are terrifying weapons attached, as they are to a huge 700lb beast. Shakespeare had probably never seen a wild boar – by the 16th century the only genuine wild boars in Britain were kept in stone walled parks and fed the lees and barley waste from beer makers – but the Bard certainly knew how dangerous these tusks were. In the poem *Venus and Adonis* Shakespeare wrote, 'and where he strikes his crooked tushes slay,' for such tusks are easily capable of disembowelling a man or even a horse. Indeed in the tale of the badly organised hunt for the awful Calydonian Boar there is reference to the fate of one Ancaeus who was castrated, with something less than surgical precision one must add, by the boar's tusks. Male herbivores and omnivores are often fiercely protective of their females and even more protective of territory. If challenged such males are often more than willing to take the battle to someone they regard as an intruder. I had come to realise just how dangerous Roly could be long before he was a year old, however.

I have never been particularly adept at bricklaying despite the fact I built my Lichfield cottage, hence, when one of my outhouse walls fell into disrepair I hired a jobbing builder to rebuild them. The unreliable nature of the Caithness workman is well known and this coupled with the fact that the Caithnessian regards outsiders as a sucker ready, willing and oh so able to be milked for money, made me settle for the services of a Lancastrian builder called Terry who was staying a while in the county. The job involved the hire of a cement mixer and it was perhaps the noise made by this mixer that triggered the outburst which was to follow. Roly at this time wandered around my croft, for he was particularly enthusiastic about eating the adders which abounded in the moorland around the house. I had, of course, warned Terry about Roly's disposition but the young man had assured me that he had worked with pigs. Roly, however, was a far cry from the fat pink porkers I had purchased from MacLeods' and I should have put him away before Terry started up the cement mixer and he came to investigate the sound made by the machine. Terry experienced what can be best described as a monumental error of judgement and picked up a spade to attempt to drive Roly away. Roly exploded and in amazement I watched the cement mixer thrown around the yard as the pig endeavoured to attack Terry. Terry was tossed into the air by the attack of the pig and for a moment at least the young man looked like experiencing the fate of the unfortunate Ancaeus.

I have never been a brave mean but I have quick wits. So after a split second's thought I seized Roly's meal bucket and hurled it at the pig, scattering the meal as I did so. Terry responded equally quickly and vaulted the half-door into my barn while Roly sought out fragments of meal which littered the yard. Amazingly, despite the fact that Roly was snorting and bristling as only a Tamworth boar can, he allowed Polly to clean his hindquarters and this had the effect of calming him a little.

However, from that moment on the scene was set for a showdown with the giant beast, and I had several warnings of the battle which was to come. While feeding his sows one day I felt Roly brush against me and glancing down saw that his tusks gashed a long rip in the oilskin jacket. I felt nothing but the rip in my jacket resembled the gash inflicted by a surgical scalpel. I believe it was at that moment I began to feel afraid of Roly and pigs are able to sense human fear and, alas, act accordingly.

Yet the showdown between Roly and myself was quite a long time in coming and I had almost forgotten his attack on me when yet another seemingly innocuous gesture triggered him to frenzy. A wet spring aided and abetted by myriad porcine footprints had reduced the pig field to a quagmire and I slithered and slipped across the field with buckets of meal, searching for the pig trough which had sunk in the foul smelling ooze, with Polly at my heels, slowly and gingerly picking her way through the mire. No one who has not lived in a peaty district or, rather, a district which sports a peaty soil, can possibly appreciate the mire a few pigs can create. Huge stones seem to vanish without trace if placed in such ooze and I have yet to find a spade I lost while attempting to dig out a submerged pig trough – which I also failed to find. Peaty soil churned up by pigs invariably develops a peculiar stench which is impossible to remove from one's clothes and now a full ten years after that time my jeans still retain just a little of the stench of that horrid peaty slime. As I approached the pig trough, wading through a full two feet of ooze, I lost one of my cheap Wellington boots and endeavoured to plod onwards with one boot half filled with slurry and a thick sock coated in unspeakable filth. From the higher, drier part of the paddock I observed Roly watching me and sensed something had infuriated him.

What triggers certain male animals to frenzy is still something of a mystery but a quite terrifying number of farm workers have been killed by bulls, boars and even rams. Ardrey believes that creatures are more likely to attack if they believe their territory is being invaded. Hartz believes that most attacks are triggered by the male's opinion his sows are being harmed. My own impression is that some males are just plain mean and take some pleasure in the action of inflicting hurt. I can remember cleaning out a bull pen for a friend of mine who had sustained a severe back injury and could not manage his small herd of Jersey cattle. As I cleaned the pen, gingerly watching for signs of antipathy from the tethered bull, I became terribly aware of my own physical inferiority and was genuinely bewildered as to how early man decided to tame the early primitive wild cattle, the ferocious aurochs which became extinct in perhaps the seventeenth century. Rumble, the small Jersey bull, watched me with interest but apparently without considering how to hurt me until, that is, I approached a certain corner of the pen. Jersey cattle, both bulls and cows, have that inoffensive doe-eyed look that is found amongst Walt Disney type creatures rather than amongst the denizens of an abattoir, but Jersey bulls are often wicked, mean creatures. Yet Rumble's expression changed little as he began to lean on me, pressing me against the walls of his pen, glancing behind him from time to time to see the extent of the damage he was attempting to perpetrate. At first I felt he had simply leaned against me by way of an accident or perhaps as a way of indicating he wanted attention but as the pressure increased I began to realise he was determined to harm me. As the air was squeezed out of my body I attempted on Herculean push and, dropping to my knees, I rolled beneath the bull while he attempted every foreleg kicking strategy in order to harm me.

Roly had no deceptive doe-eyed look and his tiny mean-looking eyes never lulled anyone into a false sense of security. As he raced towards me I became terrified of the almost evil expression on his face. What precipitated the attack I will never know but never have I been more frightened. His long yellow tushes seemed to have increased in size as he rocketed towards me and I made a furious attempt to extricate myself from the mire and run. My efforts were futile, however, and Roly's charge sent me hurtling face first into the mire.

Quite suddenly Polly galvanised into life and attacked Roly with a fury I had never associated with the bitch. An eighty pound geriatric German Shepherd Dog bitch is of course no match for the ferocity of an enraged 700lb Tamworth boar and glancing behind me as I lay face down in the run, I saw Polly hurled perhaps six feet in the air as Roly shook his head to shake the bitch off his muzzle. Twice more she rushed at him and he hurled her away from him with contemptuous ease but she continued to bark and snap at him thereby allowing me to make my escape over the barbed wire fence and into the brook which ran alongside the field.

Minutes later Polly joined me, her fur balled with mud and pig urine, panting with exertion, a rib or so broken but otherwise unharmed. I lay full-length in the icy stream, my breath coming like the blast from a traction engine and a dull pain raging in my chest and down my left arm. It was a full hour before I recovered enough to limp, now barefoot, to the house and collapse near the fire, my face and clothes caked in unspeakable filth which Polly attempted to clean off with her tongue.

When I had regained some of my breath and the ache in my chest and upper forearm had subsided a little, I began to contemplate the scenario which had almost killed me. Roly's attack was unpremeditated, or rather, I could see no reason for his frenzy, and minutes before Polly had been cleaning his ample hams in the way she had mothered him when he was a weaner. Yet at the moment of the attack Polly's protective attitude towards the giant pig had changed and she had attacked it with a totally untypical fury. She had been visibly shaken by the encounter but attempted to clean my face with loving care as I lay there contemplating the reasons for the attack and her astonishing display of fury towards the giant pig.

It was never safe to turn one's back on Roly ever again and as he grew older he grew more truculent and irritable. He also grew more and more obese and his great size was responsible for his demise. The autumn following his attack on me it rained incessantly causing the pig field to turn to the vile smelling slurry I have previously described. Roly kept to the elevated part of the field, slashing at pieces of fence wood and rendering meal buckets to pieces of plastic within hours of feeding. He still came to the wires when Polly appeared and allowed the bitch to clear the spume and slaver which dripped from his mouth, for she had returned to cleaning his face and rump within hours of her defence of me.

One day I found him lying on his side in the muddy part of the field, unable to rise to his feet. By dint of a gigantic effort and the use of three square posts I managed to lever him up whereupon he stood awhile as if pondering his relationship with me, while Polly cleaned the filth from one side of his face. The following day he had returned to his position in the mud and this time I was unable to lever him to his feet. Reluctantly I telephoned John Waters, our local gamekeeper, and requested he shoot the poor devil to put him out of what was quite obviously distress. I hadn't the courage to stay and watch John destroy the beast for despite my fear of him I still had memories of the tiny, dancing, friendly, red piglet I had bought from Hoy a few years previous. So I believe did Polly. After John had performed the deed Polly and I went to see the old juggernaut who lay still as though in a deep sleep. Polly nuzzled the old devil's nose and face and attempted to clean his face and bottom. There are probably scientific explanations to explain her odd behaviour but I swear I detected just a hint of sadness in her expression.

Epilogue

Polly aged rapidly that winter and became incontinent. I tried so hard not to show displeasure at her 'mistakes' but she nevertheless became very distressed. She looked so old, so battered and so geriatric that one night I checked her age and the date I purchased her. She was eleven years of age, no great age for a terrier, a bearded collie or a greyhound, but elderly for a German Shepherd Dog. Polly no longer leaped to her feet when I reached for the peat bin to venture out on the moor and stayed on the pier waiting for my return when I sailed out to check my creels. Once when my engine broke down and I arrived back at the harbour two hours late I found Polly up to her belly in the shallows, too tired and weak to clamber out. If she could have spoken she would have said, 'Be a man. Have the courage to put me to sleep and end my misery,' but I have never been a brave man and have never had the courage to put an old friend to death. So Polly lingered on, a pale shadow of the dog she once was, elderly, infirm and probably not enjoying her twilight years.

It would be a pleasant ending to this book to say that one night she died in my arms, but it would be a lie, a damnable lie. I dread leaving the kennels and the stock to be cared for by someone who doesn't know them, for to do so seems to invite tragedy. Indeed, any time I have left the kennels in someone else's hands I have experienced a tragedy or near tragedy. One day, however, I accepted an offer to give a talk in Norfolk and employed the services of a young man to care for the kennels in my absence. The talk was little short of a disaster and I vowed never again to address a meeting of louts with an interest in lurchers and longdogs. Shortly after the talk I received a telephone call from my kennel minder who stated that Polly had failed to rise from her bed and that her eyes had a curious sunken look. I suspected that she had experienced a stroke and my fears were confirmed when two hours later the young man telephoned again to say Polly was dead.

I had expected the worst but somehow was amazed to hear of the old lady's death, for she had been a part of my existence for eleven long and sometimes difficult years. I requested the young man bury Polly on the moor near the spot where in her later years she spent time basking in the pale summer sunlight and when I arrived home I found the place strangely empty and devoid of company.

Goodbye old girl. My kennel is thronged with your descendant, some of whom even resemble you a little. Not one has been your equal!